IMITATION OF LIFE

Preparing for the Real World
Via Creative Theatrics

Rob Simon

Copyright © 2018 by **Rob Simon**

**IMITATION OF LIFE: Preparing for the Real World
Via Creative Theatrics** / By Rob Simon

All rights reserved. No part of this publication may be reproduced, distributed or transmitted in any form or by any means, including photocopying, recording, or other electronic or mechanical methods, without the prior written permission of the publisher, except in the case of brief quotations embodied in critical reviews and certain other noncommercial uses permitted by copyright law.

Although the author and publisher have made every effort to ensure that the information in this book was correct at press time, the author and publisher do not assume and hereby disclaim any liability to any party for any loss, damage, or disruption caused by errors or omissions, whether such errors or omissions result from negligence, accident, or any other cause.

Adherence to all applicable laws and regulations, including international, federal, state and local governing professional licensing, business practices, advertising, and all other aspects of doing business in the US, Canada or any other jurisdiction is the sole responsibility of the reader and consumer.

Neither the author nor the publisher assumes any responsibility or liability whatsoever on behalf of the consumer or reader of this material. Any perceived slight of any individual or organization is unintentional or coincidental.

The resources in this book are provided for informational and inspirational purposes, only, and are the intellectual property of the author except where otherwise noted. Care has been given to credit any sources not attributable to the author somewhere within the text if not in specific annotation.

Neither the author nor the publisher can be held responsible for the use of the information provided within this book. Please always consider the safety of participants in programs you may design—whether of performers or audience members, or passers-by.

ISBN: 978-1-954302-03-7 (Paperback)

Interior Design by FormattedBooks.com

"The important thing for you to know right now is that *you* can make this happen, and there are a whole bunch of people who would love it if you did!"

—Rob Simon

CONTENTS

Introduction vii

Chapter 1: Art Imitates Life: a.k.a. Mimesis 1
Chapter 2: Classic Theater, Film, Music and More 9
Chapter 3: Imitation of Life Part 1 – The Movie 23
Chapter 4: Upward Bound Times Two 29
Chapter 5: Improv Training.. 49
Chapter 6: Imitation of Life – The Training 61
Chapter 7: Processing 81
Chapter 8: "The Back-To-School Special" 91
Chapter 9: The Wichita Griots Cultural Arts Camp 105
Chapter 10: Buckner TAPS (Teaching the Arts
        Performing School) 123
Chapter 11: Improv Revival – Start Strong Wichita 137
Chapter 12: Creative Theatrics: Why You, Why Here,
        Why Now? 149
Chapter 13: Life Imitates Art 159

Getting To Know Rob Simon 173
Index... 175

INTRODUCTION

We all have experiences from which we gain significant knowledge. That's life. However, even if we lived a record-breaking number of years for a human life, we could never experience everything from which we could gain useful knowledge that comes from direct experience. *Indirect* experience, on the other hand, significantly extends the possibilities of what we can learn by witnessing what happens to others—whether in real life or in scenes imagined and produced as theater.

Science asserts that our brains can barely distinguish between real experience and that which is imagined or intuited. Why not take advantage of this in creative ways that extend our understanding of the human experience? We can witness various occurrences, and even discuss them, and this gives us a view of the real world reflected through the arts from which we can learn and grow. It's imitation… mimicry…a process called *mimesis*, and it is powerful.

With this "Imitation of Life," performers grow, and audience members grow as they are engaged, entertained and inspired; and what is created on a stage might very well become what people live in everyday reality. In fact, this type of growth happens inadvertently all the time.

But what if we intentionally used aspects of the arts to address the torrid pace of change in a way that helped us learn at a pace more commensurate with the speed of society's transformation? The alternative is to proudly possess information and ideas that may well be inadequate for our survival and fall even shorter from the threshold of our ability to thrive.

Fortunately, the possibilities for how almost any of us can pursue such an intention are endless. In addition to our real-life experiences and those of others, we have access to classic theater, film, poetry, music, advertisements, books, periodicals, fine art presentations, and so much more. All of these are potent seeds for nurturing creative theater and harvesting its fruits.

What is <u>un</u>fortunate is that many of us downshift our learning modes when we exit from structured educational settings. Unless we are retraining for the requirements and expectations of our work and careers, we often err on the side of believing, perhaps, that we already know what we need to know to experience fulfillment. Young people, thankfully, are not as prone to this conceit and thus are willing to not only experiment, but to teach based on the insights they gain from their creative trials. This is why much of what we will learn here comes courtesy of young learner/teachers. This is also why we will explore the fact that what we see staged is not necessarily what we will fully get unless we have a chance to engage in a process to discuss it and compare notes. The element of discussion is how we can ultimately use this strategy to prepare for successful living and arrive more readily at a condition we might call excellence or flourishing.

Last, let me say that there are reasons why I wrote this book and why you have picked it up. You might well be one of the persons who can carry on the traditions explored here in a way that can improve the world right where you are and perhaps far, far beyond the locations you can directly impact. There is no better person than you, no better place than where you are, and no better time than now.

IMITATION OF LIFE

If you want to share my optimism on these points, turn the pages and let me tell you about ordinary people who have achieved extraordinary results with what we are calling "Imitation of Life." We will explore the synergy between life and art and help you to use each to expand and enhance the other…and, in the end, the lives we all live.

Rob Simon, 2018

"Fyodor Dostoevsky predicted that at first art would imitate life, then life would imitate art, and finally, that life would draw the very reason for its existence from art."
—Ravi Zacharias, Can Man Live Without God
(Dallas: Word Publishing, 1994) p. 73

"Hold, as 'twere, the mirror up to nature, to show virtue her own feature, scorn her own image, and the very age and body of the time his form and pressure."
—William Shakespeare (Hamlet -3.2.23-26)

"As long as you keep one foot in the real world while the other foot's in a fairy tale, that fairy tale is going to seem kind of attainable."
—Aaron Sorkin

"Often the magical elements in my books are standing in for elements of the real world, the small and magical-in-their-own-right sorts of things that we take for granted and no longer pay attention to, like the bonds of friendship that entwine our own lives with those of other people and places."
—Charles de Lint

"I want you, as a reader, to experience what I experience, to let that other world, that imaginary world that I have created, tell you things about the real world.
—Terry Brooks

"Mathematics is a place where you can do things which you can't do in the real world."
—Marcus du Sautoy

"We need to give our children safe opportunities to experiment with life."
—H. Stephen Glenn

"All the world's a stage, and all the men and women merely players..."
—William Shakespeare, from *As You Like It*

CHAPTER 1

Art Imitates Life: a.k.a. Mimesis

Think of touching moments that have shaped you.
    It might have been a birth, a death, a moment with a mentor, a near-miss disaster, falling in love, or being self-convicted by the realization of a wrong you have done. It could be an epiphany, a costly mistake, the first time experiencing a self-induced alternate state of consciousness or being physically attacked. It could be getting married or divorced, witnessing something traumatic, or laughing so hard that it makes you weep, or being completely and publicly embarrassed by something beyond your control…or maybe by something for which you know you are completely responsible. You may have been bullied, ostracized or ignored, or you might have been the one who did this to another person.
    The possibilities are endless, and there is no doubt you can think of some of your own if you try. So, for just a few moments, do exactly this!
    Now, think of how such a moment could be recreated for others in the shortest possible time frame—not so they live through the same things in reality, but so they can experience them vicariously, watching these experiences unfold before their eyes in a way that

allows them to identify intellectually and emotionally with them. Video is one way to accomplish this, but assume you have no money, no time, and no equipment or materials. Assume you have nothing but a space and a handful of willing volunteers.

Are you thinking about something theatrical? A skit, maybe? A dance or a mime? The telling of a story? Charades grounded in symbols? If so, this is perfect! You're on the right track, and if you stick with me, you will become a pretty creative locomotive.

Think of actors of any size, any shape, any age from about nine or ten upward, and any level of experience or talent. They just need to be able to take direction. Now imagine how you or someone else could work with them briefly to create a reflection of the same powerful moment that you experienced, to share with an audience—perhaps one that doesn't even know they're an audience until you tell them. And, yes, it's okay if the audience actually lives through the same encounter or incident that you did, as long as no one is injured or traumatized. You can even plan for these contingencies.

Now, imagine that these people could reflect back to you and to each other about their perspectives regarding undergoing the same or a similar experience. Maybe they had a different experience, which is also okay. We are not all touched, moved or shaped in the same ways by the same things, but we can understand when some of us are stimulated differently.

Now imagine making it possible for you (and people you can influence) to create a semblance of the same life-changing event for many more people than you could ever reach on your own.

Can you see it? Could you do it? Could you replicate your experience, or the significant happenings of the lives of someone other than you for an audience? I absolutely believe you *can*, and perhaps you should!

It doesn't matter whether you are a teacher, a retiree, a housewife, a pastor, a teen leader, a theater director, a volunteer, or none of the above. If you can see this vision, you can do it. You can make it happen. You can create it with a shoe-string budget, or none at all, with as little as five minutes of planning with your volunteers—as long as your vision is clear and you are good at giving instructions. And if you doubt your ability to do this, chances are good that you know someone you can inspire who has the skills you think you are lacking. All you have to do is keep reading.

This book is meant to make visible your capabilities for affecting positive social change through creative performance on stage. Making the effort to do what we have been imagining is incredibly worthwhile. It comes down to this: if the experience you are choosing to reflect moved *you*, or shaped *your* life, it can also move or shape someone else, especially if the occurrence is deeply and widely shared and discussed. It's all because of a process called ***mimesis***.

mimesis - mə'mēsis/ *noun/formal technical*

1. imitation, in particular...
    - representation or imitation of the real world in art and literature.
    - the deliberate imitation of the behavior of one group of people by another as a factor in social change.

In one of the quotes at the beginning of this chapter, when Sautoy proclaims that "mathematics is a place where you can do things which you can't do in the real world," he might also be speaking for movies, a magician's illusion, imagination, and maybe auto-tuning on the latest hit pop song. He probably does not speak for theater, however. Theater *is* the real world in more ways than one.

To begin with, theater is most often a *reflection* of the real world, even when it is a fanciful story brought to life on the stage, such as Peter Pan. And if an actor is sick, injured, or absent, the role she or he plays is fulfilled by someone else—just like in the real world when your car has to be fixed, your hamburger made, or your trash picked up. And when Peter or Spiderman flies on stage, or Jesus ascends into the heavens, or a witch disappears, we know it's just smoke and mirrors. Literally, sometimes. And when it happens, we will do one of two things: either suspend our disbelief and enjoy the illusion, or ask ourselves, "How'd they *do* that?!" But we always know it's real—*live*, as we say. And in many cases, it is real enough that when we walk away, we do so with the feeling that we could have been part of the production somehow, or that we benefitted from what we saw.

Then, again, maybe not. The story could be one by which we are entertained but not enlightened. It could also be one to which we do not relate at all. After all, unless it is an historically accurate depiction, it probably emerged from someone's imagination, and we don't all imagine—or experience—things the same way. And that brings us to why you probably picked up this book in the first place. If this is about "creative theatrics," the obvious question is: "Whose creativity are we talking about?" The answer is, of course, yours—or that of someone you know or can recruit to help create the audience experiences you may not, yet, feel confident you can produce.

You Can *Do* This!

Chances are good that you've either had experiences from which you and others can learn something useful, or you *know* or can identify someone who fills this bill. If either of these scenarios are the case, then you are perfectly poised in a location from which creative theater can emerge.

But you don't know anything about theater, you say? No problem. There are lots of people who do, and tons of books you can read and classes you can take to make up for that deficit if you choose. That's not nearly as important as having an audience, a message or lesson for them, and a way to reflect it on stage.

Excuse me? You are a seasoned thespian? You know theater backwards and forwards, and have even *created* plays and/or musicals? Great! Then you are already standing on third base and either need someone else to hit a single, or you need to pick a moment and steal home on your own to score with a new idea.

But let me ask you something: Do you even want to do this? Do you *want* to find a way to imitate life on stage in a way that helps others learn or grow? You do? Great! Then you have come to the right place. This book can help you do just that. You might not make any money, though.

Don't get me wrong. You *can* make money fulfilling this mission, but the folks who most need this experience just might be those who can't afford to pay for it. Then again, they may be able to pay it forward. It's also possible that someone who cares about them would pay to see them grow or expand. I mention this just in case you are interested, but what I'm sharing with you is not about money at all. In fact, if you choose, you can make some pretty fabulous things happen without a single nickel being exchanged—and, in certain cases, maybe even with only about a nickel's worth of time.

When it comes to target audiences, maybe it's a student body population at a local school that is struggling with the age-old problems of bullying, disrespect and miscommunication in peer groups. Maybe it's the staff that works with them every day. Maybe it's the parents who are pulling their hair out or getting prematurely gray trying to deal with overwhelming pressures.

Maybe it's a congregation struggling to maintain relevance or more clearly define what it believes in an ever-changing world. Maybe it's a workforce at a small plant that is having difficulty understanding everyday dynamics of working together for a common goal, while experiencing a diversity far more complex than the obvious things they notice regarding ethnicity, gender, or political spectrum. Maybe it's a single department within a large corporation.

Maybe it's a group of people who couldn't be listed in this limited space even with all the imagination in the world. The fact is that *you* know who needs to see themselves on stage in a way that helps them become a better version of themselves as individuals, and as members of one or more groups—or maybe you are just intrigued by the idea. That's why you're reading this, and *that's* why this book was written. If someone else had already created and made immediately available the perfect theatrical vehicle to inspire the people you care about, you wouldn't be reading this book. You would just be buying tickets, or hustling your charges into a theater to see some amazing play, dance, musical, skit, concert, or video that is just what the doctor ordered.

In your case, it either doesn't exist or it's not readily available—but you, ma'am or sir, may be just the person to create the perfect imitation of life for an audience that needs it.

Mimesis

That brings us to this juicy little word: *mimesis*. From the definition introduced a few pages back, we are talking about a "representation or imitation of the real world in art and literature." It's one or more stories you create to reflect some slice of life from the real world that you (or someone else) can observe. You do it in a way that is "the deliberate imitation of the behavior of one [real] group of people by another [comprised of REAL actor/performers] as a factor in social change" for your entire audience—including the performers, and those who will hear stories about what you produce.

But here's the kicker: it doesn't have to be an epic story that details a hero's journey to redemption (although that might be nice, too). No, this could be a thirty second skit, well-acted, and delivered as "interruptive theater" at a moment when it is least expected by your target audience. But it's when people get to talk about it afterward that the real magic happens. It's a little gem of focused conversation called *processing* that really makes the experience most memorable… especially if it is a *well-facilitated* discussion. However, informal independent debriefing is good, too. We'll get to all that a little later.

The ABC News magazine feature entitled "What Would You Do?" is an example of interruptive theater at its finest, complete with a pretty credible version of processing afterward by the crew who films the <u>act</u>…and the <u>reactions</u>.

Oh! You have *no idea* what a beautiful can of worms you just popped open by picking up the book you have in your hands.

We'll get a chance to explain or outline *all* of this stuff before you finally put this book down, but the important thing for you to know right now is that *you* can make this happen, and there are a whole bunch of people who would love it if you did.

But let's recap and emphasize what we are outlining so far.

Art Imitates Life

First, there are occurrences in everyday life that can be pretty accurately reflected in theater—the good, the bad, and the ugly—and it can be done in a way that allows audience members to recognize that what they are seeing on stage is real and relatable. Secondly, even if members of the audience are observing a world on stage that is fundamentally unlike their own, they could still identify with the struggle or experience of one or more characters in relation to other characters in the story or scene—and you might even inspire someone to create their *own* world to be more or less like the one they see on stage, if that is your goal. And third, if you do your homework, you can avoid any concerns about an audience disconnecting with your intentions.

What you are ultimately after is a translation of what author Terry Brooks talks about in terms of the written word, using the phrase, "experience what I experience," and to let the "world that I have created tell you things about the real world." And though it is an experience lived vicariously for your audience, you are giving them a safe opportunity to experiment with life, and to experiment with the real world. And if you involve the right individuals as *performers*, and choose or design your structure intentionally, the experience on stage will not be vicarious at all, but an immersion in a world of theater that can translate directly to the theater of the world.

After all, the bard was right when he said, "all the world's a stage," and all of us are players. However, he didn't have his character, Jaques, mention anything about the "writer-director."

In *this* case, that would be *you*!

"The whole of life is just like watching a film. Only it's as though you always get in ten minutes after the big picture has started, and no-one will tell you the plot, so you have to work it out all yourself from the clues."
—Terry Pratchett, *Moving Pictures*

"It starts so young, and I'm angry about that. The garbage we're taught. About love, about what's 'romantic.' Look at so many of the so-called romantic figures in books and movies. Do we ever stop and think how many of them would cause serious and drastic unhappiness after 'The End?' Why are sick and dangerous personality types so often shown as passionate and tragic and something to be longed for when those are the very ones you should run for your life from? Think about it..."
—Deb Caletti, *The Secret Life of Prince Charming*

"Everything I learned I learned from the movies."
—Audrey Hepburn

"People don't read any more. It's a sad state of affairs. Reading's the only thing that allows you to use your imagination. When you watch films, it's someone else's vision, isn't it?"
—Lemmy Kilmister [Interview in The Independent, 15 October 2005]

"Movies will make you famous; Television will make you rich; But theatre will make you good."
—Terrence Mann

CHAPTER 2

Classic Theater, Film, Music and More

The TV show "Mork and Mindy," about an alien visitor, was the launching pad (pseudo-pun intended) for the career of the late comic Robin Williams, and the year was 1980.

Mork has crash landed his egg-shaped space vehicle on earth while on a cultural fact-finding mission, and basically has been adopted by a single girl named Mindy while he tries to contact his home planet and get help to return.

One morning after they have shaped a friendship and a temporary life together, Mork is reading the newspaper and comes across an ad for the "Committee to Clean Up Boulder." Thinking it's an environmental group, Mork shows up to get involved and finds out they are a group of prejudiced people who want to clean up Boulder by getting rid of Polish people (among others). What they really care about is not ecology but discrimination. Nevertheless, Mork in his naiveté decides to join them, and manages to convince the group of his purity and that of his companion, Nelson, who is Mindy's cousin, and the leaders agree to meet them at Mindy's apartment the next day.

When Mindy learns the group's true purpose, she is understandably upset, shares that she and her cousin, Nelson, are part Polish and asks the group to leave. She actually is upset enough to ask Mork to leave, too, because he has started to tell ethnic jokes, not realizing their true purpose as a weapon by hate groups. Later, Mindy takes the time to explain the situation to Mork (which is her modus operandi in the show) while they are out together, but when they return to her apartment, it has been ransacked. Mindy and her cousin are now clearly targets of the hate group.

After deciding that such behavior cannot stand unchallenged, Mork returns to the Committee's headquarters and does a little ransacking of his own using telekinetic skills that are part of his heritage from his planet, Ork. Mindy finds him there after the damage is done, and points out that he has behaved as poorly as the group that attacked them. Contrite, Mork asks what they should do instead and Mindy says she was always taught to meet hate with love and understanding.

About that time, Committee members show up dressed in Klan-like white robes and hoods and discover Mork and Mindy amidst the vandalism Mork was responsible for creating. Bent on teaching Mork and Mindy a violent lesson, the group prepares to attack them. Mork then tries a version of the love approach with a kind invitation that clearly makes no impact, so he tells Mindy it may be time for some understanding, instead. In the next moment, he works a little more of his Orkan magic and suddenly "rearranges their DNA" as he explains to Mindy a bit later.

Instantly feeling a noticeable change in themselves physically beneath their costumes, the group members start to remove their hoods only to discover that the all-white appearances they expected to have were suddenly everything from black, Asian and other ethnicities to green and blue skinned.

In the group's moments of surprise and confusion, Mindy and Mork easily make their exit, but not before Mindy asks if they would stay the way Mork had altered them to appear. His response was, "Only until they learn about brotherhood without the hood."

News...or Nascent Prophecy?

In the world we live in today, there are still people who believe their particular color, race, ethnicity, heritage, religion, political beliefs or a combination of these, makes them somehow superior to their fellow humans and they seek to subjugate, ostracize, minimize, or destroy those unlike them. As of this writing, the news is full of exactly these kinds of current events. And the other folks—those who would be the targets of discrimination—would likely *love* to have Mork's capabilities. But, alas, that is not to be…at least not in real life. In theater, however, the illustration and the lesson are quite possible. As a Russian Proverb aptly points out, "Repetition is the mother of learning!" This is a lesson that needs to be repeated…until we get it. We could say that the imagined "Committee to Clean Up Boulder" has morphed into the all-too-real hate groups of the new millennium. Sometimes television foretells the future.

The Mork and Mindy show is available to buy or rent, and it would surely include Episode #45, "The Night They Raided Mindski's," a spin on "The Night They Raided Minsky's," (pronounced the same way) a 1968 musical comedy. Very unlike the Mork episode, it is a film about an accidental burlesque act directed by William Friedkin and produced by Norman Lear. There might even be some market—especially since we have now lost the genius of Robin Williams—in which the show is even available on air in syndication. Either way, it is important to realize that the story can be told, and beautifully demonstrated on stage, using theater. This can be done without much more difficulty than it took for me to tell you the story here.

And there are so many stories to tell—similar ones, and different ones.

Dragon to Butterfly

For example, there is a fascinating true story about a very unlikely friendship between a Jewish cantor, and a Ku Klux Klan Grand

Dragon in Lincoln, Nebraska. You can read about it in a book entitled *Not By The Sword*, by Kathryn Watterson.

The story begins in 1991, when Cantor Michael Weisser receives his first threatening phone call from Larry Trapp, Grand Dragon of the White Knights of the Ku Klux Klan of Nebraska. But the Cantor, with the support of his wife, Julie, decides to not be intimidated, and soon courageously sets out to meet hate with love. The Cantor actually goes to Kentucky Fried Chicken, buys a bucket meal, brings it to Trapp's doorstep as a peace offering, and basically says, "We need to talk."

This spectacular offer of friendship is how the story begins, and the rest of the book details the evolution of a relationship that went from would-be enemies to long-time friends. The unbelievable transformation included a poignant end that found Weisser the person Trapp most wanted at his bedside as he declined and died from a terminal disease.

Could this story be a nascent prophecy for where the world is headed if we learn to look for common ground rather than invest so much in our battlegrounds? I'd like to think so. But if not this one, how about the one you will tell?

In this chapter, the intent is to plant seeds of ideas about how easy it is to glean theatrical themes from classic stories that have already been told in theater and film, whether on television or in movies, but also in books, oral histories, and even in music.

I first heard the story of Weisser and Trapp in a folk song by David Roth (not David Lee Roth of Van Halen fame). The song is called "Dragon To Butterfly," and the opening lyrics pick up the story near its end before flashing back to begin retrieving some of the details of how it began:

> It was early September in Lincoln, Nebraska
> Two friends were conversing at dusk on a porch

IMITATION OF LIFE

One was all wrapped up in blankets and pillows
The other an old overcoat

Affection was easy to witness between them
The physical closeness, the tender exchange
The one in the coat gently stroking the other
Who struggled but managed to talk just the same

He said, "Do you remember the day we met, Michael
I heard you were coming and I called many times
I didn't want someone like you to move in here
I wasn't used to your kind

But instead of returning my ignorant curses
You just kept on answering the phone
And you knocked on my door with a bucket of chicken
The first time you came to my home

The two men were laughing now, shaking their heads
With a sense of the passage about to take place
"Larry, if someone had said we'd be friends
I'd have called them insane to their face

But you can't always tell what's inside of an apple
And you can't always trust what you see…"
And Michael continued to wonder out loud
After Larry had drifted to sleep

CHORUS
How a man can move mountains, a world can be turned
And the greatest of distances easily spanned
When the strength that's invested in making a fist
Is transformed into shaking a hand…

The idea of this kind of digging for theater topics, alone, could be a book of its own. I just thought you would find some of my favorite scenes and stories from my theatrical mining excavations as inspiring as I have. And the inspirations are never-ending if we are motivated to look. Ideas keep popping up for me all the time…and I am not exceptional in this regard.

From Fantasy to Fulsome Experience?

I have this recurring fantasy of me (or some other performer or presenter) being able to snap a finger, and make the venue that holds an audience go pitch black in an instant—so dark that you couldn't even see your own hand in front of your face. After what would surely be a dramatic gasp-inducing pause, I think it would be moving to facilitate taking advantage of this hypothetical environmental blackness to make a salient point about how ridiculous it is to presume we can judge others by their appearance.

I say "hypothetical" because today's pocket technologies could have the whole room illuminated in less than thirty seconds. But in such a theoretical dark room, appearance would <u>dis</u>appear, and if we were to judge people at all, it would have to be by something other than the way they look. Of course, the deeper fantasy would be to even take away the ability to notice differences with our other senses, too. *Then* what would we judge? Only the content of another's character, I imagine.

Here's the thing, though. With the right kind of theater experience, my fantasy could be made real. We could separate audience members from the senses they normally depend on to be discerning in the world, and force them to interact based on what emerges from a person's insides rather than get caught up in the particulars of their outside packages.

Theater has a magic all its own—particularly when the audience is immersed in the experience rather than being a passive attendee.

IMITATION OF LIFE

This fantasy even inspired a song...or vice versa? I'm not sure what came first, "the chicken or the egg," in this metaphorical case. But here are the primary lyrics to a song I composed called "No Difference In The Dark":

There is no difference in the dark
And your arrow has missed the mark
If you think you're more than me in the Eyes of God.
Take away the <u>differences</u> we see,
Then you'll agree with me.
You will find we're like each other after all.

Sometimes our problem is we see too well.
Sometimes we don't see well at all.
I have a revelation I must tell!
I'm not afraid to stand up tall!

If we see black or white;
If we see day or night;
If we see different words,
Or believe lies we've heard;
If we see blonde or gray;
If we see blind or gay;
And then think hate's okay;
Then I just have to say...

There is no difference in the dark...

If we miss love and dreams;
If we miss mixed up teams;
If we miss common ground
That lots of us have found;
If we miss peace for war;
If we miss who we are;
Then we are much too far
From seeing love's bright star!

There is no difference in the dark...

There are things we look at all the time,
And a lot don't matter very much.
If we could see what's inside you and me,
If we could feel what we can't touch,
Then we would know...

There is no difference in the dark...

Venus, the Science Teacher

And *now*...before we get too far afield...to briefly explore another one of my favorite TV vignettes of all time (and as an educator, I *love* this one) we take a quick peek at Venus Flytrap and "The Atom in Two Minutes." This one comes from a very entertaining show from bygone days called "WKRP in Cincinnati," which ran from 1978 to 1982. Some gray-haired readers will remember this show...probably fondly.

For the uninitiated, though, "Venus Flytrap" was the on-air moniker for a terminally cool African-American disc jockey played by actor Tim Reid in the ensemble cast for the show. The episode we will discuss here finds an old friend of the DJ showing up at the radio station to talk to Venus because she—also African-American—is concerned about her teenage son who is skipping classes at school and has started hanging out with gang members. She pleads with Venus to talk to her son, and he graciously agrees (probably thinking, "How bad can it be?") and that he might even do some good.

So, a meeting is arranged at the radio station and the kid shows up...with two homeboys in tow that look to be about six-foot-two and two hundred and twenty pounds each...and he is pretty buff himself. Venus is momentarily taken aback at the menacing trio but simply asks if the two homies would give him time alone with his friend's son, and they agree and leave the studio.

IMITATION OF LIFE

Once alone (to make a longer but cool story short) Venus reflects to the kid that his mom is concerned about him, and feels him out about why he is hangin' on street corners rather than attending classes according to his worried mother's wishes. The kid responds by saying that when it comes to school work, "I just don't get it."

When Venus asks him to elaborate with an example, the young man says, "Like the atom, I just don't get it." He has apparently been in class when the structure of atoms is being taught in science, and it doesn't make sense to him. Venus then makes a wager with him, asking if the young fellow will honor his mother and get back to school if Venus can teach him the atom in two minutes. The kid smugly agrees, erroneously thinking it's an easy money bet that he can win.

Venus grabs a handy marker and commandeers a wall to create an illustration where he draws a circle to represent a neighborhood that's "a whole lot of nothing." He then populates a hangout in the neighborhood called the Nucleus with a gang called the New Boys who eventually team up with another group called the Pros: "Really positive cats…because they have all the women." But there is another gang outside the neighborhood called the Elected Ones who are "some really negative dudes" and they are always circling around the neighborhood looking for trouble. By the time Venus explains that all of the gangs adopt the term "Tron" (which Venus tells him means "dude" in Swahili, a white lie designed to impress him) and that the New-Trons and the Elect-Trons always make sure they have the same number of gang members for safety's sake, he has pretty much metaphorically represented the structure of an atom. Then his new protégé passes Venus's test by correctly naming all the parts of an atom, and basic important relationships and characteristics within and between them, because he now understands it all in a vernacular he knows well: the world of street gangs.

This quick outline doesn't quite do the lesson justice, but you can see it for yourself in less than five minutes by looking up the clip on YouTube. The best teachers are often the ones who can translate new concepts into familiar metaphors and analogies. Then, much like in this TV show illustration, lessons come alive in completely new ways.

There are so many instructive and inspiring moments in the storytelling of film, novels, songs, and more. It's the kind of thing that happens when Richard Dreyfuss's lead character tells the red-haired female clarinet student he is teaching to "play the sunset" in Mr. Holland's Opus; or when Will Smith's caddy character tells Matt Damon's golf prodigy character to "see the field" in The Legend of Bagger Vance; or when the teacher played by Robin Williams takes his students from the classroom on their very first meeting for a spontaneous field trip to the hallway to help them "seize the day" in Dead Poet's Society; or when John Lennon sums up the capriciousness of life in the song "Beautiful Boy" that is an ode to his son, Julian, in a single powerful line: "Life is what happens to you while you're busy making other plans."

What is really awesome, though, is how scenes like these are ripe for reflection in creative theater endeavors, or they become seeds for brand new pieces that can make the same or similar points.

The Fugitive and The "Lying" Nun?

Although Harrison Ford and Tommy Lee Jones starred in a great reprised version of the story in 1993, I personally felt "The Fugitive" was David Janssen in classic TV from the mid-sixties. What a great protagonist to root for…Dr. Richard Kimble, a nice guy who lost his beloved wife to murder, and then (adding notorious insult to injury) was wrongfully charged with the crime! Armed primarily with the knowledge that a one-armed man was somehow responsible for his wife's death, Kimble escaped from custody when a train derailed and set out to prove his innocence while being wanted everywhere as…a fugitive.

Again, for our purposes, we'll point to a particular episode. Officially it's in the fourth season, Episode 19, "The Breaking of the Habit." (If you choose, you can watch the show by searching for it on YouTube, or http://www.tv.com/shows/the-fugitive-1963/the-breaking-of-the-habit-36741/.

IMITATION OF LIFE

Kimble is seeking the help of Sister Veronica, a teacher at a Catholic school whom he has already befriended. This time, he needs recovery time from a gunshot wound, and also asks for her help with transportation to find the one-armed man. He has evidence of his presence in the area at a café, and he is sure the two of them can find him.

Along the way, they have two encounters with police officers—once at a roadblock while Kimble is hiding in the trunk, and another when Sister Veronica is stopped by an officer for running a stop sign. In both instances, the sister engages them in conversation, and the officers draw their own erroneous conclusions.

The first time, an officer says, "You are all alone?"

Her response: "My religion teaches that we are never alone."

The officer says, "I see what you mean," and goes on with a little more small talk before letting her drive on. She really doesn't answer his question, but he either takes her response as an answer, or decides it doesn't matter because he can see there is no one else in the car with her…or both…or neither.

The second encounter is a little more dramatic. Kimble is riding in the front seat with the Sister driving (having discovered an exhaust leak that was seeping into his hiding place in the trunk) and when they are stopped, he has her pull over next to an alley in case he needs to try an escape on foot. When the officer starts engaging Sister Veronica, she tells him (among other things) that she is from the school, and a bit later the officer asks Kimble…who never makes eye contact with him…"Are *you* from the school?"

At that point, the enterprising nun takes over and the rest of the conversation basically goes like this:

Sister Veronica: Officer, if you don't mind, we are in a great hurry…Father Taylor has a toothache, and his dentist is here in Tarleton.

Officer: Oh.

Sister Veronica: It's all the peanut brittle he eats. I keep telling him and telling him, but after all the priest is a man…and you know how men are.

Officer: Yeah, I guess…Good luck with that tooth, there, Father.

Later, Kimble says to the nun, "I'm grateful for what you did," with the implication that she had lied on his behalf. The sister responds by saying, "I didn't say you were Father Taylor. He did. I said Father Taylor has a toothache, which is true, and I said his dentist is here in Tarleton, which is true. Of course, I dare say it'll take a little straightening out in the confessional."

When I saw this episode as a youngster, I was struck by two things: one, how easy it is to jump to conclusions based on too little information, and how often people do so rather than being more inquisitive; and two, how valuable and sometimes necessary it is (and difficult it must be) to be creative enough to maintain integrity when you are between the proverbial rock and a hard place in terms of your honor. These lessons have stayed with me for a lifetime, and I find myself still studying them after all these years. And where did they come from? Essentially, they came from one scene in a single episode of a TV series. And how many ways could the same lesson be reflected to an audience?

These lessons…and others…can be taught in as many ways as there are creative people to attempt them.

"Beneath the surface of *Imitation of Life* lies the reality
of what [Director, Douglas] Sirk rightfully believed
was a seriously deranged American society.
—Ed Gonzales, 2003

"In Lana Turner's biography, she writes about the making of [Imitation of Life]. It was made shortly after her daughter stabbed Lana's gangster boyfriend to death. She said that when you see her crying in the funeral scene, those tears were real. When Mahalia started to sing 'Troubles of the World,' all of her troubles started to come back to her and she got up and ran out of the church. They had to run after her and bring her back to complete the scene."
—smrhyne, 2003

"IMITATION OF LIFE is one of those rare films that gets better every time I see it. I guess that's because it's important on more levels than you can take in on a single viewing. I could go into how it's also about a single mother's struggle for independence in 1950's male dominated society. I could argue that it's not as sappy and melodramatic as it's reputed to be. I could argue that John Gavin's performance was better than a lot of people say. However, I think I'll save those discussions for when I see it again."
—Jon Noel Shelton, 2005

CHAPTER 3

Imitation of Life Part 1 – The Movie

The main title of this book rings a bell for some readers. It is the same as a classic movie that you may have seen. It's one of the best of all time, in my opinion, and frankly part of the inspiration for not only this book, but a training course that bears the same name. There will be much more about the latter in Chapter 8.

It is worth noting that each of the new millennium reviewers quoted above are talking about a 1959 movie classic that was remade from a film first screened in 1934. When you do the math, that is a minimum of over 58 years ago, with the original hitting the screen 25 years before that. And why do I point this out? It is to start by making the case that this kind of longevity for a film is the very definition of classic. To go further, though, is to explore why the film bears this title, and what the connection is with this book having the same title.

In the movie, it is 1947 and two single mothers—one black and homeless, the other white, a widow, and an unsuccessful actress—take their daughters to Coney Island. The aspiring actress is Lora Meredith, and she meets Annie Johnson when Lora's six-year-old daughter, Susie, gravitates to Annie's eight-year-old daughter, Sarah Jane. When the playmate alliance is discovered by the mothers, soon there is a resonance between the two very different women, followed by an invitation from Lora to have Annie and her daughter share the small apartment she occupies with Susie.

Over time, we learn that each woman has challenges with their daughters. With Annie, the problem with Sarah Jane is that she can see the differences between the experiences of people based on skin color, and doesn't want to be black. Then, because since she's light-skinned, she starts passing as white as soon as she figures out that she can. Her mother, however, is heartbroken that her daughter begins an estrangement from her to protect the ruse, and Sarah Jane behaves despicably in the process—which also makes Annie feel ashamed.

With Lora, the challenge is that she sees her daughter almost as an inconvenience, because of her own determination to make it as an actress, and basically ignores her in in her compelling effort to be a star. This is partly why she wanted the other woman as a live-in companion, but they actually become close friends.

Meanwhile, Lora has a love affair with a photographer named Steve Archer and he proposes marriage. Lora brushes him off, however, because her ambition to become a star on Broadway is her top priority. She neglects Steve as much as she does Susie.

While the light-skinned Sarah Jane continues to reject her painfully heartbroken mother in her effort to pass as white for her friends, Lora starts to achieve success in her career, and stardom is right around the corner.

Ten years later, she reconnects with Steve by chance, but is soon off to shoot a film in Italy. Steve pays attention to Susie while Lora is on location in Italy, and by the time she returns, she decides marrying Steve is a good idea, but Susie—a young woman now—has also fallen in love with Steve.

Meanwhile, Sarah Jane's secret has been discovered and her cultural house of cards comes crashing down—especially with the young man who had been her beau until the secret was discovered. He vehemently rejects her, and Sarah Jane runs away from home and a life of lasciviousness, and works to make her way socially and professionally. Her mother remains determined to pursue a family ideal with her daughter which embarrasses Sarah and (she feels) holds her back.

The climax of the film occurs when Sarah Jane learns of her mother's death while she is away and barely arrives in time for the funeral. Having made it just in time, she obviously regrets their estrangement, and is painfully distraught at how poorly she has treated her mother in an effort to create her own idealistic life, but there is no longer an opportunity to make amends.

So What Is the "Imitation of Life?"

Thomas Caldwell writes in 2008, "While the title *Imitation of Life* on the surface seems to be referring to the artificiality of Lora's glamorous career that takes her away from her daughter, the title is perhaps more of a sly comment on how racism in 1950s America denied African American people the life that white people took for granted. Sarah Jane's self-loathing at being African American and having an obviously black mother also leads her into an imitation of life as she estranges herself from [her mother] Annie in order to pass as white and therefore not have to suffer the indignities of discrimination."

We could also make a case that Susie's life was an imitation of what it might have been had her mother been less neglectful; and there is the possibility, too, that her being smitten by Steve was a veiled attempt to imitate that aspect of the life her mother was living. Finally, we could ask if the life Annie lived was the one she wanted, and probably easily conclude that it was not and that her experience, as well, was an imitation of the one she would have preferred—certainly with her daughter, and perhaps with her own new love interest outside of the mysterious nearly white father that we never really learn about.

Ultimately, this film has so many layers to examine in terms of (as Caldwell puts it) "…conflict within the home [and a story] about emotional anguish, love affairs that go wrong, unrequited love and life-threatening situations…love, death, social standing, loose morals and heartbreak…[and] passive and unintentional racism."

On this latter point we could examine Sarah Jane's roommate assuming that Annie is the maid, and Lora commenting that she had no idea Annie had so many friends. We can also find rich irony when we learn that Annie has always owned a mink coat, where Lora was lent one early in her career so she could appear dressed for success with the upper crust.

Are People Still Imitating Life? And Can We Help?

Today, we must wonder how much of the lives people live everyday are imitations of the real thing. Based on this classic film and current events, we could ask what is the true nature of racism today versus in the 1950s? And what about sexism, ageism, and modern feudalism or unspoken caste systems? How do today's young people preserve family of origin while making their own way in the world…or do they? What has social media done to the authenticity of human life? Have we forgotten how to interact face-to-face with legitimacy?

How often do people work at passing for something or someone they are not, especially in the age of social media distortion of world views? How many of us live lesser lives than we can imagine because we don't feel we deserve them or that we are capable of them? How many of us are living lives that someone else wanted for us rather than living lives that are commensurate with our true purpose? How many of us are "model humans" in the sense that we are cheap imitations of the real thing?

Is Ed Gonzales correct to say that Director Douglas Sirk *rightfully* believed we have a seriously deranged American society? Can we create our own Mahalia Jackson moments to get people in touch with their own "troubles of the world," in the same way that Lana Turner was confronted with hers? Do single mothers still struggle for independence, dignity, survival, respect…and lives that are fulfilling? Have we had enough of a male-dominated society yet… or one dominated culturally and economically by Europeans and their descendants?

I don't claim to know the answers to these questions, but I am certainly willing to ask them. I know and practice encouraging others to ask these kinds of questions—either overtly or covertly—from the stage. And when we do so, it gets people talking about the answers to such questions, and coming up with versions of them that inform the decisions we make every day about how to show up in the complex world we live in. And *this* is the beauty and power of creative theater.

Some of us are not only capable of uncovering or creating epic stories, but we find a way to do so for the sake of audiences. And yet, epic stories are not necessary for the kind of learning and inspiration that many of us need. Give most of us time to think about it, and we can tell a story about someone who is caught in the trap of an imitation of life rather than living their life authentically. We could write it, tell it from the stage, make a video, pen a poem or song, or create live theater. And as surely as we do, someone will have an opportunity to measure their own efforts at day to day living with the tape measure provided by some other person or persons we can observe in the stories told. When we do, perhaps we can save ourselves from the same kinds of mistakes and avoid a personal episode of the imitation…the mockery…the faking…the pretense…maybe even a parody or distortion of real life. At the same time, we create a more genuine experience for ourselves, and maybe even for others we care about.

This book is your invitation to create a genuine experience that you and others can delve into with gusto as it unfolds on stage, but this will not be a passive experience. Oh, no. The witnessing of scenes and dialogue is just the beginning. It's what happens afterward that really makes the magic happen, and we will get to that in due time.

For now, though, we have examined a movie classic that inspires many more questions than answers about who we really are as we show up in the world each day, and what kind of world we are creating…or destroying…each time we do so.

And, are there models for this kind of creative theater that we can examine? Oh, yes! There most certainly are!

"I didn't have time for talent shows and stuff like that.
I was into books and studying real hard."
—Cheryl Lynn

"Magic mirror on the wall, who is the fairest one of all?"
—The Queen - *Snow White and the Seven Dwarfs*

"It is an absolute human certainty that no one can know his own
beauty or perceive a sense of his own worth until it has been reflected
back to him in the mirror of another loving, caring human being."
—John Joseph Powell, *The Secret of Staying in Love*

"I define connection as the energy that exists between
people when they feel seen, heard, and valued; when they
can give and receive without judgment; and when they
derive sustenance and strength from the relationship."
—Brene' Brown

"Allow yourself to be an anchor and anchored by others."
—Asa Don Brown

"True faith is a risk worth taking. Always keep hope
and faith in your heart. Anchor yourself."
—Akiroq Brost

"I can choose to sit in perpetual sadness, immobilized by
the gravity of my loss, or I can choose to rise from the pain
and treasure the most precious gift I have—life itself."
—Walter Anderson

"Everything negative—pressure, challenges—
is all an opportunity for me to rise."
—Kobe Bryant

"Live as if you were to die tomorrow; learn as if you were to live forever."
—Mohandas Gandhi

CHAPTER 4

Upward Bound Times Two

It started with casual conversations, which led to a respectful friendship and eventually morphed into a job offer, which then became a grand experiment.

He was Carl Foster, the young director of a nearby YMCA. As an even younger classroom teacher, I supervised creative extracurricular activities at a junior high school right down the street with kids who would often spend after-school hours at the Y where he worked. It was just a matter of time before we would meet and become acquainted. And it was not long after our inevitable initial acquaintance and quick friendship that Carl's different role as Executive Director of the Upward Bound program at nearby Wichita State University led to a dialogue about the summer component of the program and a way that I might be able to contribute.

Upward Bound's summer session was to feature classroom workshop sessions on a variety of academic subjects to provide remediation and/or acceleration for underprivileged high school students being encouraged to go on to college. Carl thought one of those sessions should be dedicated to the performing arts, primarily as a vehicle for developing self-confidence and, of course, to have some fun as well. He thought I would be a good candidate to facilitate that track for six to eight weeks. I happily accepted his offer to take the task on.

We Could Do A Talent Show...

The easy first thought was, "We could do a talent show." But, just as quickly, I dismissed the idea because I had attended too many boring and poorly organized talent performances where mediocre abilities outweighed the bright spots. Knowing that one of the main goals was to have every student in the program involved, I couldn't even generate excitement in my own mind for the vision of a spectacle featuring a herky-jerky pace courtesy of a Master or Mistress of Ceremonies thrust into the position with too little guidance for how to play the role. I knew that I could teach and train the right kids to play key roles in logistics and management, and even get better performances from amateur performers who may have had little or no experience on stage—but still, a talent show didn't seem compelling enough to generate real excitement. Unless…

"What if we made it a theme show?" I asked myself. What if we assessed the interests and abilities of the students with a talent survey and had them devote themselves using their strengths to support a theme? What if every song, every dance, every skit, every *anything* was dedicated to a message that would entertain and enlighten our audience, and maybe even inspire the performers themselves? What if kids who would rather die than be on stage performing could write, or work stage crew, or manage the house during the performance? What if, as a team, they could design our marketing materials and print media, or hustle up resources we wanted to use as stage props or set pieces?

Dang!

I was on to something, and I knew it! But what theme would be useful? The possibilities were endless, but with relatively little time to think it through, prepare the class structure, and actually be face-to-face with the group for the first time, I knew I would have to have all my ducks in a row and at least one serviceable idea for a theme before actually meeting the "performing arts class." Soon, the muses started dancing in my head, and an idea started taking shape. In the simmering pot of my thinking, I tossed in a little wondering about their talents, a little inspiration from amusement parks, a bit of fairy tale magic from the wicked witch in the Snow White story, and the ace in the hole of all the supporting roles non-performing students could play, and a vision appeared.

Magic Mirror

I settled on a theme for a show that would be called "Magic Mirror," with the title being representative of a visual and metaphorical set piece that would be our vehicle for introducing talents during the show. This would also be used to encourage everyone involved including our audience to find a way to uncover hidden talents and abilities, just as we would be doing with the class project. And then, one of the muses smacked my creativity with a two-by-four, and an "old inscription" for the "magic mirror" came shining through:

> **Mirror, mirror, cut and buffed and polished by an elf,**
> **Unearths hidden dreams and things forgotten or unknown.**
> **He who looks inside this glass can see inside himself,**
> **And find a gem within him that has been there all along.**

A script for the show would have to introduce the mirror somehow, and the mirror would have to play a part in how talents were woven into the show. The biggest challenge would potentially be whether the students would be inspired by my vision enough to make it their own. I had a good feeling about the possibility, but I wouldn't truly know until I could paint a verbal picture for them and see how they would respond.

When the moment came, I was excited to discover that as I laid out the theme show vision as part of my synopsis for the class, the students seemed as captivated as I was, and voted overwhelmingly to adopt it as the structure for what we would create, and how we would work together to accomplish it! With that hurdle overcome, it was time for them to complete talent surveys and to get started on weaving a storyline together with talents, and performance pieces that would support our theme. We were off and running on the first day!

I handled most of the scene scripting the first year. That seemed easiest with the aim of establishing a strong baseline for the project. I didn't know how much pressure the students would be able to handle with such a new undertaking, and I was also aware that some would repeat their participation the following year and would be able to take on more creative responsibility with a summer's experience under their belt.

The setting for our inaugural performance was an amusement park and the show opened with a scene that featured two big guys hauling a crate into a House of Mirrors where they would install its donated contents from a rich eccentric into an empty space. Once the new "mirror" installation is finished, both workers notice there is no reflection from the mirror's surface, and think it's weird. One worker then notices the inscription which he reads aloud. The other guy discounts it as a "crock," and announces he's headed out to lunch. The first worker, however, is mesmerized by the inscription and finds himself suddenly thinking aloud that the park is auditioning for a new dance troupe, and he has always wanted to be part of something like that. He decides he will audition at the next opportunity, and leaves the stage. The next time you see him, he is dancing…with all the other performers who wanted to be in a dance routine for the show.

A second scene features a mother leading two kids into the House of Mirrors by the hand, and while they are amused by the usual distortions, mazes, and infinity arrays, their mother is struck by the inscription on the Magic Mirror. The audience hears her proclaim that she has seen a flyer advertising a fashion show being organized at the park, and that she still has her "figure," and maybe she should look into that. Soon, she gathers up her children and exits the attraction, but you see her later in the show…modeling a lovely outfit with other fashion models.

IMITATION OF LIFE

    Incidentally, for the fashion show, the stage crew moved two small stairstep units and a platform which was arranged between them in a matter of seconds while the stage went dark between scenes. We only used the curtain at the opening and closing of the show. Otherwise, we used all light stage/dark stage transitions, and the crew did their amazing, speedy, and quiet work with only the ambient light left on stage when focused lights were extinguished. The crew had also been part of a group that located those items from a nearby business that was getting rid of them, realized they might work for a fashion show runway, and helped to transport them to the venue.

    And so, the show unfolded with other characters encountering the "magic" mirror. Though it was clear that all of them noticed there was no reflection, and thought it strange, those who "found a gem within them" were the ones who invested in the inscription and committed to giving themselves an opportunity to express their gifts. This, then, became part of the show—whether the characters performed alone or with others.

    A bit of narration along the way likely filled in any gaps in the message we hoped to convey. The show was a hit with the audience, and every student had one or more important roles to play. They were engaged in expressing themselves through acting, dancing, singing, modeling, and working as crew, or perhaps in managing the theater's guests as greeters, ticket agents, and ushers. All students had roles to play in pre- and post-site logistics such as marketing, printed program creation, transporting props and set pieces, and cleaning up afterward and loading out what was brought in for the show.

We couldn't have been happier with the way everything turned out for our first attempt at producing a theme show, but as anticipated, this was only the beginning. The next summer featured a new show and some new students as well as previous students.

Connection

I really hadn't planned the show we did during the second summer that I taught Upward Bound's performing arts class. In fact, I almost didn't offer my idea for the show at all, because it didn't leave a lot of room for the students to create content. However, the greater truth is that I was excited about an amazing inspiration that had come to me in the interim since the previous summer session, and I knew Upward Bound would be a great laboratory for producing the show…if the students were amenable to the idea. So, I mustered my courage, hoped for a minor miracle, and shared my ideas for a show for which I had already developed a theme, about seven songs—complete with sound tracks—and beginning ideas for scenes that could introduce or incorporate the songs.

Fortunately, the students fell in love with the theme and the songs, and we were immediately on our way with additional writing, casting, sequencing scenes, and rehearsals for a show. The core of it had come to me in one fell swoop of inspiration as I sat in a living room all but oblivious to a raucous party swirling all around me.

It was a celebration with friends and colleagues of a successful concert we had put on, and there was a lot of excitement as we reveled in the joys we had created for performers and audience alike. For some reason, I zoned out after a while, and in that meditative space, ideas started to germinate—in a completely random and unexpected way, it seemed.

Maybe it was all stemming from a subconscious realization of what had been and was happening throughout the evening, and even before then. There are lots of possibilities that have occurred to me in retrospect, but in those moments, all I could do was notice what was bubbling to the surface of my awareness.

When the inspiring ideas wouldn't let go, I interrupted one of the hostesses long enough to ask her if she had a piece of paper and a pencil I could use. And as if to offer additional affirmation for the power of what was coming through unbidden and in what seemed like the oddest circumstances, she actually brought me a tiny little book with blank pages. With the pen she also brought, I wrote a familiar quote on the first page: "Nothing is STRONGER than an IDEA whose TIME has COME!" Then, beginning on the facing page, I began to write down what was coming through...as a continuation of the message that started on the first page:

'cause THIS is ours:
<u>CONNECTION!</u>

Next, in a creative blur, came song titles on the same page:

"Let's Get Plugged In"
"Love"
~~Electricity~~ "ENERGY"
^{What} God IS
Infinite, Radiant One!
Positive Rhythm
Transformation Nation
Mental Traffic
"PEACE"

THANK GOD

This last line was not so much song title as it was a benediction, at least at that moment. (It *did* become a song later.)

On the following page, I wrote a few random but connected notes about possibilities. Afterward, I quickly scribbled this core message, an articulation of the inspiration coming through:

If there is a
RHYTHM to the UNIVERSE
WE as part of that
UNIVERSE should
never lose TOUCH with
the <u>RHYTHM</u>!

If there is MEANING,
If there is UNDERSTANDING
If there is KNOWING
We Should...
KNOW!

If there is LOVE—
and surely there
is—then we must
become LOVE and
it must be US.

If all of EXISTENCE
has a FOUNDATION on
which it is built, then
may we always be able
to find a firm footing
on that foundation.
If there is GOOD,
or RIGHT or PERFECTION
or HARMONY, let us
never be apart from it.
And if that which binds
us together one with
another and unto our
selves can be called
SPIRIT, then may
we always be ONE with it.
And if that which
gives CREATION its
LIFE can be called
ENERGY, may it always
prove to be the life of
each of us.
And if the POWER

that IS is EVERYTHING
without us as we are
NOTHING without it, and
if that POWER is
the LIFELINE to which
we should always be
attached and from which
we draw the BREATH that
makes us who and what we are,
then may we always
seek to find and
Never lose our
CONNECTION.

And if none of these
things are anything
apart from GOD, then

So be it.

In the debut of the show, many of the song titles actually became songs. Other songs for the show (and for alternate projects) emerged later from seeds that seemed to scatter like dandelion tufts from this original message rather than from the list of titles.

One thing I firmly believe is that most of us have open conduits to the ultimate source of creativity, and if we can ever slow down long enough to tune in, we can actually pick up broadcasts (if you will) from the universe. Of course, the next most important steps are to actually trust that the inspiration is there for a valuable reason, and then choose to share it or work to help it blossom.

Take a moment right now and consider what inspiring thoughts you have had along the way that might be the seed of something wonderful!

Anchor

We began in season three with the usual orientation for the class, and engaged in discussion about the previous season's show with the one- or two-year veterans' abilities and recollections playing a large part in offering firsthand accounts and memories of our inaugural and second-year projects. Then, true to my intent, I offered only a theme and provided no initial scripts for scenes. I did, however, have a new original song that I created to support the theme (assuming it passed muster with the class) which was for a show that we would call "Anchor."

The students liked the theme, and as our discussion continued, we agreed that we wanted to demonstrate the importance of the anchors we have in life that help keep us grounded such as family, work, religious belief, education, or a romantic relationship. Also, we wanted to play with the idea of the difficulties that can arise when a person does not have an anchor or loses one they've come to depend on.

There were a number of students who were interested in writing scenes, so we organized them into work groups and got them started on ideas. Meanwhile, other students started brainstorming song lyrics and music for possible dance routines to incorporate into the show.

One student who was interested in writing decided to work alone, and he ended up creating and co-starring in the third-year show's most dramatic moment opposite a young woman who was actually visibly pregnant at the time.

Their scene opened with him in bed, in the dark, and snoring. An alarm clock goes off, and he reaches out from under the bed covers and angrily slams it off. He lays there for a while, and his wife starts to call to him from off stage and fuss at him about staying in bed so long, and then starts to add in a whole list of things she needs him to attend to. Obviously irritated, he starts to go through the verbal motions of acknowledging what she is saying as he sits up, swings his legs over the side of the bed, and turns on a bedside lamp.

Apparently not getting the response she wants, his wife comes into the bedroom to add the last few items she wants him to handle, and he manages to convince her that he has everything under control. Satisfied for the moment, she leaves the bedroom to head back to her kitchen off stage, leaving him alone sitting on the side of the bed.

After a few moments of sitting there silently, we see him open a drawer in the nightstand. He takes out a pistol, looks at it, and puts it back. After a few more moments of him quietly demonstrating a certain amount of angst, he repeats essentially the same movements with the gun, but places it on top of the nightstand instead of back in the drawer.

Again, he sits quietly for a few more moments with body language that screams dejection and defeat. For the third time, he picks up the pistol, looks at it, and then points it at the side of his head. In the very next second, the lights go black, and he pulls the pistol away from his head and squeezes the trigger. It is actually a track official's starter pistol, and the loud retort draws a collective gasp from the audience. As they catch their breath, however, a narrator's voice in the darkness delivers a short but meaningful speech to encourage the listeners to look out for those who might be in danger of destroying themselves or others because they end up without the anchor or anchors they need to keep themselves grounded and strong.

After that narrative, the lights come back on, and the bedroom has given way to a simple set change and a carefully placed follow-up scene, which launches a closing series that eventually leads to the final song, the show's theme song. The lyrics send the audience out with this message dedicated to them:

> **Verse 1**
> **All my troubles are not hard to bear.**
> **When I need strength, I find it in the things that touch me**
> **Such as love, understanding and care**
> **And the comfort of knowing God is there.**
> **So when life shakes me up or makes me spill my cup,**
> **I don't worry about a thing;**
> **I just hold on to something that makes me strong.**
> **I find an anchor.**

Chorus 1
Give me an anchor!
Give me an anchor!
Give me something to hold on to!
Give me an anchor!

Verse 2
When you understand what makes people tick;
Or accept a gift from someone that makes you happy;
Or recover from having been sick;
Or there's some other problem that you've licked;
If someone cares for you and the things you do
And you believe in who you are,
These are the things that make you strong.
You've found an anchor.

Chorus 2
You're my anchor!
You're my anchor!
I am glad for the strength of my life!
You're my anchor!

For a moment, let's stop to consider the three main goals that underlie projects that fit the "Imitation of Life" paradigm. One is to offer opportunities for growth for the performers. A second is to entertain and enlighten, inspire and educate an audience. The third is to reflect real life through the arts in a way that can inform how we LIVE life IN the real world.

When students had an opportunity to offer feedback after "Anchor" closed, these were among the comments submitted:

> "I really enjoyed being in performing arts. It was a nice experience. I really learned a lot of things about myself that I didn't know I was able to do. I found out I am able to write plays, able to act, [and] able to

write a song. I didn't know I was able to do that but now I do. I believe our *Anchor* production delivered the message we intended to deliver to some of our audience."

—*Carla D.*

"I used to be shy to be on stage but now I'm not."

—*Carla S.*

"I think *Anchor* did what we wanted it to. All we asked of it was to say that there are things we need, and what they are. The show said that, and much, much more. It was truly enjoyed by cast, crew, and perhaps most notably, the audience. This, I think, is the most important thing, next to making all of us think about the things we were saying and doing.

—*Susan R.*

"I definitely enjoyed the class this summer as it helped me to discover my talents as a writer. I definitely improved my performing arts skills in the way of my acting skills, i.e., I learned how to do a stage slap, and my monotone has departed slightly.

—*Stuart S.*

"Next year, I think we should start the advertising a little earlier, but there's not much more that we could do to make the show all that much better."

—*Tonya H.*

Still, I Rise

When the fourth summer session began, I simply told the story of what we had produced in the previous summers, invited any returning students to add their own comments, and asked the class to brainstorm themes they might like to build a show around for the third year. I started a timer for a few minutes and encouraged them to toss out ideas as quickly as they could while I wrote them all on a chalkboard.

During the session, one young woman blurted out, "Still, I rise," and it rang a little bell in my memory, but I couldn't quite place it at that moment. However, when the brainstorming period was up, and the group felt we had enough ideas to choose from, we launched into the clarifying stage. I asked the young lady to say more about the idea she had tossed out. She told us, "It's a poem by Maya Angelou," and she quoted part of it. When the class heard her clarification, they quickly decided that they liked her theme the best and adopted it. Then the work began in earnest—including my own because I had created nothing for the show, and since the theme was newly adopted, neither had anyone else. We knew, however, the poem would be part of what we would deliver:

> **STILL I RISE**
> BY MAYA ANGELOU
>
> You may write me down in history
> With your bitter, twisted lies,
> You may trod me in the very dirt
> But still, like dust, I'll rise.
>
> Does my sassiness upset you?
> Why are you beset with gloom?
> 'Cause I walk like I've got oil wells
> Pumping in my living room.

IMITATION OF LIFE

Just like moons and like suns,
With the certainty of tides,
Just like hopes springing high,
Still I'll rise.

Did you want to see me broken?
Bowed head and lowered eyes?
Shoulders falling down like teardrops,
Weakened by my soulful cries?

Does my haughtiness offend you?
Don't you take it awful hard
'Cause I laugh like I've got gold mines
Diggin' in my own backyard.

You may shoot me with your words,
You may cut me with your eyes,
You may kill me with your hatefulness,
But still, like air, I'll rise.

Does my sexiness upset you?
Does it come as a surprise
That I dance like I've got diamonds
At the meeting of my thighs?

Out of the huts of history's shame
I rise
Up from a past that's rooted in pain
I rise
I'm a black ocean, leaping and wide,
Welling and swelling I bear in the tide.

Leaving behind nights of terror and fear
I rise
Into a daybreak that's wondrously clear

I rise
Bringing the gifts that my ancestors gave,
I am the dream and the hope of the slave.
I rise
I rise
I rise.

Maya Angelou, "Still I Rise" from *And Still I Rise: A Book of Poems*. Copyright © 1978 by Maya Angelou. Used by permission of Random House, an imprint and division of Penguin Random House LLC. All rights reserved.

Later, I would add a theme song with these lyrics:

Chorus
Still I rise!
No matter what life does to me,
I'll rise
Because
My destiny insists
That I rise.
I'm meant to live above the clouds.
I'll rise
To reach my goals.

Verse 1
Rare is the one who can live a life of ease
And never worry about a thing.
Life has a way of dishing out low blows;
And sometimes we want to just give in.
But I'm determined
To always
Give life my best shot;
And to face things
With courage

And to reach with all I've got!
I may get knocked down,
But I'll stand up
And give it one more try.
Until I breathe no more
I want to always say…

Chorus

Verse 2
There can be times when we live some of our dreams;
And maybe we can earn a crowd's applause.
But we forget there are other worlds to find
And get trapped in the glories of the past.
I want to always
Remember
The stairway that I climb
Keeps stretching onward
Although I
Keep on leaving steps behind.
I may accomplish
Many things
That I set my mind to do,
But I won't stop there;
You still will hear me say…

Chorus

Special
Still I rise! I'm rising up!
Repeat three (3) times)
Still I rise!

© 1985

Living for Tomorrow

Now, I must make a confession. The title of the show for summer number five is essentially all I remember or have a record of us having produced. We started with basically the same kind of class orientation as we had before, telling the story of previous summer session productions. However, from the moment students were asked to brainstorm ideas for the theme until the show was completed, the students were in complete control except for stage direction. Otherwise, all of the writing, singing, dancing, acting and casting was done almost exclusively by the students.

Their theme, "Living for Tomorrow," was about making decisions in the present that would tie into goals set for the future. Their independence as a team was a perfect reflection of the evolution I hoped they would make from my having produced most of the show the first year to almost none of it the fourth and fifth years.

I could not have been prouder of how the program evolved over the five years it was operational. The students were not only Upward Bound in terms of their additional preparation for college life and work, but the Imitation of Life paradigm was off to a very good start, and also upward bound!

"What happens in improv is you create your own storyline."
—J. B. Smoove

"In improv, the whole thing is that it is a relationship between the two people, as a back and forth."
—John Oliver

"The improv, sometimes it works, sometimes it doesn't, but when it does, it's like open-field running."
—Robin Williams

"The kind of improv that I'm particularly addicted to is the kind that…aims at creating a momentary, fragmentary experience that has a totality to it."
—Del Close

"Improv plays such a huge role in finding great lines—you'll be surprised at what comes out of your mind inadvertently. A lot of times it's better than a script you've worked out ahead of time."
—Nick Swardson

"You know how sports teach kids teamwork and how to be strong and brave and confident? Improv was my sport. I learned how to not waffle and how to hold a conversation, how to take risks and actually be excited to fail."
—Emma Stone

CHAPTER 5

Improv Training

Improv Training. That's what it was called for short. The official full title was Improvisational Teen Theatre Training, and alternately it was known as Improv Training for Substance Abuse Prevention…because that was one of its major focuses. But for those who were a part of this phenomenal learning experience for 25 years, it was nothing short of magic.

Imagine you are a teenager from somewhere in the state of Utah, and you show up at a ski lodge in the summer with maybe five to 10 young group mates and an adult sponsor or two. You are greeted by a group of people much like yours who cheer for you as you exit your vehicle, carry your bags for you, and escort you to your rooms in the lodge. Then you have a little time for relaxing and acclimating before a dining hall dinner and a first gathering of all participants and staff.

Maybe you heard stories about this camp. Maybe it was all new to you, and you had no idea what to expect. But one thing is for sure, you can tell it's going to be unlike anything you've ever experienced. Little do you know, not only will you be pleased, but you will likely leave at the end of the week as a different person than you were when you arrived. And you will have access to an exciting new tool for change, as well.

ROB SIMON

With your materials, you receive a notebook chock full of information, and on the first page, you see this:

Welcome Cast Member!

We are ready for the show to begin. The cast is assembled, the scene is set, the prompters and directors are ready and the stage manager's hand is on the curtain.

Congratulations on being chosen as part of the cast. We are all looking forward to working with you. You have been cast in a production that has great potential to change your life and the lives of others in a way that will bring rave reviews. You have been selected because you care about and can become a positive role model for others.

Our call times are exact. Our rehearsal schedules are rigorous. Break times are for relaxing and getting to know the entire cast.

Rehearsal time is almost here. You will be trained, coached, and nurtured throughout the entire gig. So, we invite you to concentrate on the moment, prepare yourself well, risk for growth, and give an award winning performance.

In your hands is your prompt book. Bring it with you to rehearsals and performances. You will be using it in the training sessions, rehearsals, and for reflecting at the end of each day.

So give yourself permission to ENJOY. It's time for the curtain! Break a leg!

Lori Hargraves, Training Director

iii
Improvisational Teen Theatre Training Inc., Copyright 1992

You soon learn that the way to interpret what the cover letter outlined is to know that the "show" is the training, the "cast" is every participant, the "production" is everything the students absorb and use for their creations, and the changes, role modeling, connections, reflections, rehearsing and coaching mentioned or alluded to will all eventually unfold in a carefully designed experience...as promised.

It is worth mentioning that this training—as brief as it was, usually occurring over just five and a half very long days—was a comprehensive process and included exposure to a great deal of information, insights, practice in relationship and community building, team-building, stagecraft, life skills, specifics about drug and alcohol use and how to prevent it, and the lynch-pin of the whole model: a piece called processing. (More about that in an upcoming chapter.)

What made it all worthwhile, however, was the culminating product. In this case, it was a "showcase scene" produced by each group on the last evening of the training experience. By the time the groups were ready to take the stage, members understood how to create at least one reflection of the experiences they knew or could learn about that related to the problems and challenges discussed, such as drug and alcohol use. They also knew how to create similar ones in the future. They could apply these insights to individuals, relationships, families, and communities...on stage...in a way that made them come alive for their audiences, and then guarantee that their audience would share perspectives about the reflections, and likely understand them, learn from them, and be able to apply what they learned.

Defining Improvisation

It is also important to note (for the purist) that *improvisation* or *improv*, as we define it here, is applied significantly more in the creative process than in the performance process. This model was not about creating a junior version of the popular TV show "Whose Line Is It Anyway?" for example, where performers were expected to spontaneously create a scene anew each time they performed. On the other hand, creative, experienced and/or well-trained troupes can and often do adjust characters, dialogue, interactions, and more to be relevant in different ways for different audiences.

For instance, if a group were performing a scene to explore the dynamics of addiction to drugs—issues relating to enjoyment, compulsion, progression, denial, and endangerment of self and others—secondary school student audiences and adults would likely be educated, mature and sophisticated enough to be exposed to specific characterizations and plots related to whichever drugs the group wanted to highlight. However, if the audience consisted of primary school children, such a presentation might be over their comprehension abilities. And yet, the same points could be made by showing a child protagonist who is addicted to cookies. A scene could still illustrate how enjoyable eating cookies is, how the deliciousness makes you want to beg for them or sneak more cookies, how you want to eat more and more cookies all the time, how you might lie about looking for more, and how you might do dangerous things to get in the cookie jar that your mom puts on top of the kitchen cabinet to keep you from getting them without permission.

Another way that improv can still be employed (after the kind of scenes we are talking about have been developed enough to be consistently replicated) is when performance circumstances change for the actors. The actors who are playing characters in a scene might change, or there may be a need to recreate a scene with fewer characters than normal—in which case one or more actors might have to insert a narrative to cover dialogue or salient points that would normally be handled by the players who are unavailable.

Finally, for now, another way that this improv model is similar to the kind of spontaneous scenes many people think of when they think of theatrical improvisation is that there is almost always no formal script. The exception to this might be when a group wants to preserve a vignette that has become a classic. Dialogue and staging might be noted, outlined or transcribed in a way that is sort of a mother dough starter for recreating current scenes that may be relevant or desirable in the future—maybe even by completely different personnel. Of course, another way to do that is to video record scenes for posterity.

Real People, Real Life

When we explore the roots of the model being described here, we ultimately find real people reflecting real life. Let me repeat that: <u>We find real people reflecting real life</u>. The reason this is important to note is that you should fully understand that it is not necessary to create these kinds of experiences using polished actors under the guidance of a seasoned director. Such circumstances could be advantageous in some ways, but it is far from necessary. In the years that Improv Training was up and running, we experienced compelling theater from young people who often had little or no experience performing on stage.

It's also not necessary to be great at *generating* stories to tell. We live stories every day, and we also know other people who do, or know *about* people who do.

Another important truth about this template is that scenes don't have to be long to be effective. In fact, some of the most powerful ones I have ever seen have been exceptionally short. A prime example comes from a troupe I directed for a few years with the Start Strong Wichita program (see Chapter 11) that was one of two performances we delivered that had only one word of dialogue. The one I will share took ten to fifteen seconds to perform, and often led to discussions that lasted ten or fifteen minutes…or more.

Imagine two performers—one male, one female—passing each other from opposite sides of the stage. They bump into one another in the middle, and the male turns angrily toward the female and venomously snaps, "Bitch!" They continue on their separate paths until they have left the stage. The scene takes just a few seconds, but when the audience is engaged in unpacking what happened and what it means, there are an amazing number of factors to examine:

- Where does the scene take place?
- If there are clues about setting, does the audience relate…or translate?
- Do they know each other, or are they strangers?
- Do they have history together? If so, what is it?
- If there is any mutual history, does it include a personal relationship?
- Is the male a chauvinist?
- Is he a bully or just an ass? Is she?
- Does he interpret the bump as intentional? As careless? Or is he just entitled?
- If this is about a disrespectful attitude toward women, why does he have it?
- Was he already angry at someone or something else?
- Was this moment IN character or OUT of character for him?
- Had she been antagonizing him before, and this moment was just his last straw?

The list of questions could go on because the way people look at this simple occurrence reflects a great number of audience attitudes, experiences, and curiosities.

Occasionally, when this scene was in our rep, after some discussion we would repeat the exact same scene—but with two males instead. Then, in addition to all the possible questions above, others would come to mind such as:

- Does it make a difference if a guy calls another guy a "bitch?" Why or why not?
- Is the name-calling just reflexive on the speaker's part based on peer influence?
- Does calling a guy a "bitch" reflect a general disrespect for the equality of women alongside men?

- Is such a moment reflective of homophobia or disrespect for LGBTQ individuals?
- And what difference—if any—does it make if it's two girls?

Can you see how a ten-second scene can really invite significant discussion…and probably some learning as well? And is this just *one* option out of *how* many possible directions we could take? The possibilities are endless!

Now let's look at a more complex example, and more emotionally impactful. We will also examine a mix of devices that performers can use.

Torn

For this scene, imagine about ten actors. Perhaps a half dozen of them…mostly male, and a variety of shapes and sizes are grouped more or less down stage right (DSR) as if just hanging out on a street corner, or in a park, or wherever. Two of them are miming using cans of spray paint, and the audience easily gets the impression that they are painting graffiti. There is no urgency, and the mood is light with smiles and laughter, and maybe a little horseplay as the group interacts.

The tallest of the male actors seems to be a character that all the others respect or like—especially the most petite of the females who is clearly connected to him…but not apparently in a romantic way. She also doesn't seem particularly connected to the activities of the others.

You barely notice the other group of actors—mostly female and clustered in a seated position down stage left (DSL), and if you pay attention at all, you get the impression that it is a scene within a home. Perhaps it is a living room or den where a TV is on and one of the females could be a mother.

Suddenly, off stage and unseen by the audience, a member of the group slams a large book on the floor, and as the loud bang startles everyone, you see the small girl in the DSR group instantly flop lifelessly to the ground. Now, if you hadn't already figured it out, you get the impression that this scene is street gang related, and you have just witnessed a drive-by shooting. The lead male actor goes to the young girl immediately, distraught and sobbing and crying out, while many of the others are dashing about as if to determine the details of what has happened and gather clues.

After a few moments, you see the lead male gather the lifeless body of the girl into his arms, and the whole group walks slowly across the stage to the DSL group where they enter the home scene, and the actor you suspected is a mom gets hysterical when she sees her son carrying the lifeless body of her daughter, and lets out a blood curdling scream followed by heart-wrenching sobs.

The son tries to comfort her as best he can through his distress and anger, but then someone in the group says something along the lines of, "Don't worry. We'll take care of this. It's time for payback."

At that point, the mother shifts instantly from her distress to her concern for her son's well-being as she realizes he is in line with this expressed strategy, and she begs him not to go. When one of the other gang members grabs her son by the arm as if to usher him out for the retaliation, she grabs him by the other arm. Then you see him clearly torn between his two loyalties...

The scene ends.

Need I say more? Opportunities for broad ranging and emotionally deep discussion unfold. This scene, when unpacked, is enormous. The whole scenario is over in maybe seven or eight minutes, and here I am recounting one that was actually performed at Improv.

And consider this: No special costumes were required, much of the action was mimed, there was very little dialogue, and no set pieces were used—except two or three chairs for the home scene. Only one low tech sound effect was employed, but it is likely you find your heart strings vibrating even though you only experienced this event in your imagination. And I'll bet your mind's eye is more than enough to bring the richness of this staged experience fully into your awareness, and maybe even in a way that you could see individuals you know recreating this scene for an audience of *your* choosing. And if that's the case, we have arrived at the reason why we are traveling back down memory lane for this peek into a deceptively simple but powerful strategy called Improv.

But let's look a bit closer.

Putting It All Together

As J.B. Smoove points out for us, in improv you create your own storyline, and it doesn't matter whether the story is borrowed from real life experience, or created from scratch based on the *understanding* of real experience. The more important consideration is why we choose to tell the stories we tell from the stage, and the "whys" are as varied as the people like us who would consider doing it. Where there is an audience or a potential one, there are possibilities.

Within your storyline, however, improvisation can be key in determining the choices you make for dialogue, or whether you have any at all. A lot can be said sometimes without saying anything. But when it comes down to lines that actually get included in the kind of scenes we are exploring, we may or may not be nearly as clever spontaneously, or in everyday life as we can be when we have an opportunity to reconsider what would be different if we could do things all over again. The good news is that sometimes we *can* do things over again, and that is especially an advantage of planning scenes like those we consider here.

Here is something that happened for me which I think is a great example of the kind of planning dynamic that can help an improv evolve during the creative process.

One morning, I stopped at a convenience store for gasoline. After filling my tank, I headed into the store to pay for my fuel and grab a refreshment. I walked between two cars parked directly in front of the store to get to the entrance. Just as I did so, the driver of the car on my right reached out of the driver's side window and dropped the plastic zipper just removed from a fresh pack of cigarettes. If I had noticed this maybe a second sooner, I could have caught it as it fell. If I had, I would have turned to the driver and asked, "Would you like me to throw this away for you?" But, alas, my reflex was not quite quick enough.

Let's say, though, that I was part of a group that wanted to make a point about litter. We could recreate this scene and buy that extra second or two, and put my question in the mouth of an actor. Then we would have an opportunity to see how the driver responds by using our imaginations. Beyond that, the conversation between two or more actors in our scene (or the lack thereof) could fuel one or more points about disrespect for the environment.

Or perhaps we wanted to explore the phenomenon of road rage. We could take this same scenario, have our lead actor and the secondary actor get into a heated exchange related to the initial gentle confrontation, and then have it continue after the antagonists are back on the road. Where does it go at this point? You tell me.

Like Del Close says, the kind of improv that works for me is the kind built on a "momentary, fragmentary experience that has a totality to it." The meaning of a moment can be so beautifully extended through theatrical devices, and then delivered to whomever we choose. Improv…and what grows from it…gives us chances to do just that. We get to explore relationships between people, between people and things, between people and ideas, between one idea and another. We can even turn ideas into characters if we want. So many options emerging from starting with an idea and seeing where it goes… or where you *want* it to go. And depending on when performance occurs, where an idea normally goes can be exchanged for a whole new direction…sort of like taking a route home from work that you don't normally take, or deliberately choosing the scenic road over the expedient or usual one.

The ultimate idea with improv is to find a way to do on stage what is done in life, and to do it in a way that is somehow familiar to those in your audience…or surprising…or attention-grabbing…or instructive…or inspiring…or whatever you or your audience need it to be. And maybe the effort doesn't make you *excited* to fail, as Emma Stone believes, but when it works, like the brilliant Robin Williams has said, it *is* like open-field running. And for those of you who are not sports fans, that translates into being able to move forward as you please with few or no impediments.

With improv, a little risk goes a long way toward creating powerful experiences so that those who witness them, and those who present them, might benefit. With improv, *everyone* gains.

But what happens if you extend the performance into other creative performing arts areas? Well, stay tuned. We are about to take another little trip to see what more is possible.

"Music is a more potent instrument than any other for education, because rhythm and harmony find their way into the inward places of the soul."
—Plato

"Whoever has skill in music is of good temperament and fitted for all things. We must teach music in schools."
—Martin Luther

"I see dance being used as communication between body and soul, to express what is too deep to find for words."
—Ruth St. Denis

"I am a dancer. I don't dance because I want to. I dance because I need to. I tell a story by the movements of my body."
—Anonymous

"If I could say it in words, there would be no reason to paint."
—Edward Hopper

"I found that I could say things with colors and shapes that I couldn't say any other way—things I had no words for."
—Georgia O'Keefe

"Art is not what you see, but what you make others see."
—Edgar Degas

CHAPTER 6

Imitation of Life – The Training

Take a look at this logo—particularly the images at each corner:

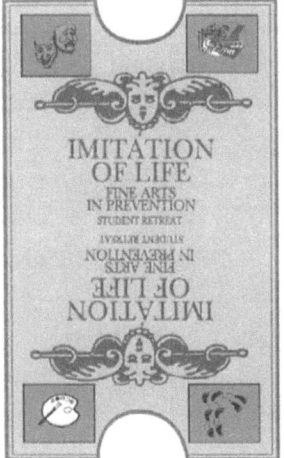

In case they are too small to see clearly, I will point out that the corners speak of theater, music, visual art, and dance. This is very intentional. Why?

Think for a moment about everything you've learned, thought about, or imagined in the last chapter regarding improv. Then notice that only one of these four avenues of expression is emphasized there…

only theater. Now, take that model, in all of its splendor…and stir in the other three. What do you have now? You have improv on steroids. You have theater cubed. You have creativity to the fourth power! You have exponential possibilities. You have just about every creative avenue that performers need—*plus* opportunities for even more!

Quick! Tell me what all of these folks have in common: George Clooney, Neil Patrick Harris, Jamie Foxx, Justin Timberlake, Amy Adams, Kate Hudson, Meryl Streep, Catherine Zeta-Jones, Jennifer Lopez, Beyonce, Prince, Demi Lovato…and others that must remain unnamed here.

If you said they are all multi-talented, you are right. These are folks who are *at least* what we call a "triple threat," which classically means that they can sing, dance and act. But depending on which one you pick for a closer look, you could find these three talents as well as others. Maybe they can write, direct, produce, compose, design fashions, play musical instruments, paint, sculpt and who knows what else.

Good for them!

But for every ridiculously multi-talented performer like these, you can probably find a hundred that are equally or even *more* talented… in maybe just *one* area, but that one area is enough. And when you downshift this whole realization a few notches to *young* people who are still *discovering* what they can be good enough at doing to make a splash, you find opportunities to help them use the talents they <u>have</u> so that they can create the theatrical and other performance features you…or they…<u>want</u>.

This was the thinking behind the creation of a "Fine Arts in Prevention Training" called…wait for it…"Imitation of Life." Yup. We went there. And sure, we can say the classic movie we have explored in these pages had something to do with this moniker, but the truth is it was the *metaphor* we were after when we selected that title—and for all the reasons we are exploring in this book.

We recognized that not every kid we could work with would be an actor or even want to say a single word on stage. But if not that, there were those who would dance until their body parts might fall off, or sing until birds would shut up and listen, or make musical instruments sing *for them*, or create images in two or three dimensions that would speak volumes without a single word or sound. With the doors open for them, any and *all* of these kinds of talents...and more...could be employed to create opportunities for performers and audiences to place life in a laboratory called theater, and dissect it until it was understood in ways that just casually looking at it on the outside could never do.

Dance and the Satin Stars

Way back in the late seventies, I was working in a school where kids could be in drama, or band, or vocal music (and, of course, sports) but there was no organized outlet for dance...so I created one. I started a dance club. They were called the Satin Stars, and outfitted in black satin overalls with white tuxedo stripes.

Not being a dancer myself (although a decent choreographer) I just had a feeling that if I opened the door, dancers would walk through...and wow, did they ever! There were some incredible dancers at Brooks Junior High School.

Right around this time, a very popular dance craze was called "The Robot." For a beautiful demonstration, go to YouTube and look for a video called "Best Robot Dance Ever!" The model of what this dance looks like doesn't get any better than what the young man in the video demonstrates...in just two minutes! You won't believe how absolutely mechanical and joint defying his moves are, not to mention the astounding strength required.

Anyway, one routine I remember that our club put together was quite the hit. We had maybe seven or eight dancers who could all robot, and I helped them create a dance routine that was a scene from a baseball game. There was a pitcher, a catcher, a batter, maybe an umpire, a couple of infield players, and a few outfielders. There were strikes, balls, swings and misses, foul balls and pop flies, an extra base hit, and a slide to safety...and maybe more...all set to funky music by dancers who made it look like they were machines playing the game rather than flesh and blood.

The point is that we might have completely missed this amazing display of dance talent had there been no outlet for it. None of my kids were in choir or band, and none played sports or were in drama, but they could dance their butts off—and they loved doing it!

With "Imitation of Life Fine Arts in Prevention Training," (IOL) the goal was to help interested student performers take advantage of their skills and talents to create experiences for audiences that were designed to awaken them to the dangers, difficulties, and challenges of choosing self-destructive or risky behaviors of all kinds, and to facilitate discussion based on what was created. But instead of just *acting* scenes out with dramatic flair, their verve could also include music, dance, and visual art—anything that could make the points they wanted to make, get people talking, thinking, and making safer and healthier choices regarding substance use.

From History to Current Events?

Now…before we go further, it is *very* important to note that much of what is being explored in these pages so far could be referred to as a history lesson, and we will note that history is about what *has* happened. Both Improv and IOL emerged at a time when drug and alcohol use among young people were of grave concern in many communities—so much so, that agencies were willing to invest in promising or useful strategies for tackling the problem. This issue may *still* be of great concern in many locales, but this does not at all preclude the use of creative theatrics to address absolutely any issue you *want* to address. We will take the time to look at other areas in later chapters of our historical exploration.

The other point to make is that the main idea in this book is to learn from the *history* in a way that can inform *current* events. If you are inspired by what *has* happened, in places like Kansas, Texas and Utah, then perhaps you can be instrumental in deciding what *will* happen. I want the takeaway to be that you can quickly and effectively move from history to current events, and change lives through the employment of theatrical experiences made rich by any and all of the performing arts, and made substantial by your grasp of the issues you want to address and the best practices or ideas for tackling them. We can move from the imitation of life on stage to the maximization of successes on real life's stage.

When IOL was first made available to education-based clients, we promoted it with the flyer you will see on a following page. At the time, with clients making decisions about whether to invest or not, everything on the page was important for their consideration. However, most importantly—then and now—were the objectives. Here, I quote them exactly:

The general objectives of **"Imitation of Life Fine Arts in Prevention Training" (IOL)** are the following:

- To introduce elements of improvisational theater coupled with prevention best practices into a school environment as a strategy for parlaying real and imagined experiences into entertaining and effective teaching tools;
- To take advantage of the power of peer influence by engaging a group of interested, creative and energetic students and one or two adult sponsors to use peer influence for positive purposes;
- To establish the IOL paradigm as an on-going practice in the school that can be replicated for positive effect as long as there are interested students and sponsors willing to make a positive impact on the school environment; and
- To positively impact academic goals by using the proven effectiveness of the arts as an enhancement to educational outcomes.

This formula still works incredibly well. The two points I emphasize differently for you are that: (1) this model is applicable far beyond schools, and (2) though it is still important, the focus does not *have* to be prevention programming. Ultimately, *any* organization or interested individuals can apply this strategy for almost any positive productive purpose.

On the second point—that the focus of IOL does not have to be prevention programming—it is still very useful to note that as we seek to address issues of importance, challenge, or hindrance, the kind of education that undergirds prevention efforts is quite useful.

For example, most prevention programs are built on at least one of these four pillars, if not more: information, skills, alternatives, and social policy. The best are built on all four. Here is a quick sketch of what these pillars represent:

1. **INFORMATION**: These refer to the established facts about the issue with which you are dealing. The facts will be different for alcohol, tobacco, and other drug use than they are for depression and suicide, or other behavioral risks.
2. **SKILLS**: These usually reflect life skills (social competencies) and include everything from goal setting and problem-solving to self-regulation, self-worth, or work ethic.
3. **ALTERNATIVES**: This category addresses the viable and attractive or effective behaviors or choices people can make that are less problematic than risky behaviors.
4. **SOCIAL POLICY**: This has to do with how society at all levels—from family groups to national or global—draws the line between what is acceptable and what is not. This is the hardest to achieve because there are so many competing ideas. However, the straighter and clearer the line, the more effectively we can know and address when someone crosses it in the wrong direction.

"Imitation Of Life"

Fine Arts In Prevention Training

A Conceptual Outline

Defining "Imitation of Life" (IOL)...

The general objectives of **"Imitation of Life Fine Arts In Prevention Training" (IOL)** are these:

- To introduce elements of improvisational theater coupled with prevention best practices into a school environment as a strategy for parlaying real and imagined experiences into entertaining and effective teaching tools;
- To take advantage of the power of peer influence by engaging a group of interested, creative and energetic students and one or two adult sponsors to use peer influence for positive purposes;
- To establish the IOL paradigm as an on-going practice in the school that can be replicated for positive effect as long as there are interested students and sponsors willing to make a positive impact on the school environment; and
- To positively impact academic goals by using the proven effectiveness of the arts as an enhancement to educational outcomes.

Pre-Training Planning

We recommend at least one session of planning before the project begins. It is important to assess needs, identify school objectives, survey potential staff sponsors, understand performer potentials, and make decisions about the building-specific design, scope of content, short- and long-term goals and outcomes for the training – as well as related performance(s), and follow-up activities.

Training Duration

The number of training sessions/days should range from three to five (or more) depending on: (1) the identified objectives; (2) whether or not the training is done in a retreat setting; (3) the length of each session/day in the training design; and (4) the number of trainers that are involved.

Follow-Up Activities

Follow-up activities can vary a lot depending on the following considerations:

(1) whether or not and to what extent a long-term, on-going performing troupe is an expected outcome;
(2) whether or not a qualified teacher/performer is regularly available as a troupe or group sponsor;
(3) what functions any follow-up activities are meant to fulfill; and
(4) whether or not the follow-up is provided by a trainer or the teacher/sponsor.

The improv model we have been discussing can effectively address all of these tenets—either through the performance, or processing afterward—and it is only limited by the skill and preparation of the presenter/performer/facilitators. An effort can be made to address gaps in any category—information, skills, alternatives, or social policy—by pointing audiences to resources where they can find more ideas. With this as an intentional strategy, there are very few limitations…if any, and the distinct advantage of the inspirational component of the arts.

With the assertion that any organization or interested individuals can widely apply this strategy for positive or productive purposes, perhaps we should examine some illustrations.

Shoplift…or Left?

Picture the following presentation delivered by a school group at one of our trainings.

A scene is set up where a young person is working the counter at a retail outlet. Two people are seen browsing or shopping. A third person is on stage but outside the audience's focus, not seemingly engaged in shopping, and with his back turned toward the rest of the action. You get a clue from the dialogue that this is perhaps a pharmacy or a convenience store.

While the clerk is assisting a customer at the counter, the second shopper appears to pick up an item and then starts walking away from the counter. The clerk notices this and then excuses himself to pursue the other person, who is now ostensibly headed toward the exit.

The clerk confronts the individual and tells her that she needs to either pay for the item or give it back or he will tell his manager. She responds by saying she can't believe he's making such a big deal about a small item, and you get the impression from the rest of their dialogue that they are acquainted and maybe even friends. The fourth individual who has just stepped into the audience's focus is now watching the exchange, but his role is not clear. Meanwhile, the customer at the counter is waiting for the clerk to return and is escaping our notice.

After some additional dialogue, the clerk retrieves the item the first customer was looking for and returns to the counter, while the young woman and the other man leave the scene together.

The end.

The next thing you see and hear is the scene's processor asking the audience to share what they observed. A follow-up discussion about shoplifting, entitlement, friendship, responsibility, integrity, honesty, and more is now underway.

Smorgasbord of Subject Matter

Now, imagine another workshop showcase scene from the archives. Four actors are scattered across the stage frozen in positions equidistant from each other and from the audience's left to right. There is one male standing and facing off stage right, and three females—one seated on the floor facing the audience, one standing with her back turned toward the audience, and the other standing facing the audience, but in a slouched and disinterested pose.

The young man unfreezes and presents a brief monologue in which he recounts having finally succumbed to his passions to have sex with a girlfriend. Now, he says he realizes that having had unprotected sex, he is now at risk because he could have contracted a disease. He decides he'd better get checked out. He returns to his freeze.

The young woman seated on the floor launches into a soliloquy in which she tells of an attractive, charming boyfriend, but adds that his "anger problem" is an issue and that sometimes "he hits me." Despite this, she indicates that she doesn't really want to leave him… then she freezes again.

The third actor opens up by wheeling around and snapping, "Stop *looking* at me! I know I'm *fat!*" The audience can tell she is *not* fat, but she then talks about how hungry she is…having not eaten in days. She also confesses that she *does eat*, and that her mom *sees* her eat all the time, but Mom doesn't know that afterward she goes to the bathroom and throws it all up. After a couple more assertions, she refreezes in her previous position.

The fourth actor also talks about a boyfriend and the great relationship she has with him and the future they hope to have together, but then admits that her friends think she is making a mistake with him, and she doesn't want her parents to know about him because she is sure they will judge him, too. The audience is left for a moment to wonder why she's having difficulties, until she also reveals that he is black…while she is obviously white…and then returns to her frozen disinterested pose.

The male actor unfreezes long enough to have a brief exchange with an imagined medical professional to ask the results. We can tell from his dejected countenance before he freezes again that the news is not good.

The seated girl wonders aloud whether she should leave her boyfriend…before she is still again. The bulimic girl enlivens just long enough to relate that her mother is worried about her now and wants her to see a psychiatrist, but she shouts, "I am NOT SICK!" The last actor reveals that she is determined, it seems, to stay invested in her fulfilling relationship, but wonders aloud why people have to be so insensitive, prejudiced, hateful, and cruel about interracial relationships.

All of the actors relax, and the male steps forward to begin what I'm sure you can clearly imagine is a rich and far-ranging discussion. This, as an audience member pointed out during processing, is the kind of scene a group could produce to begin to address a number of pertinent issues in a relatively short time frame. The advantage of such a scene is its flexibility in terms of content, and its broad-based appeal. The biggest <u>disadvantage</u> is that it could conceivably lead to a lot more discussion than the available time would allow, and perhaps open up difficult issues that could not be adequately addressed in the allotted time.

This is a good opportunity to discuss the importance of knowing your audience, carefully choosing your material, being prepared for anticipated difficult questions, comments, revelations, or stories if the content is controversial, emotional or especially difficult. It is also important to think ahead and make sure resources are available either on-site after performances, or with recommendations for follow-up information or assistance. (We will talk more about some of these items in the next chapter.)

Emotional Whiplash

Let's examine a third scene that introduces a couple of added elements to kick off examining the many others that are possible.

First of all, we again see the strategy of having two or more clusters of actors to represent different areas, time frames, or mindsets. We will now peek at one in which the scene opens with a male and female actor seated side by side facing the audience. We soon learn through action and dialogue that they are in her car, headed to her house after a date. She is complaining to him about how her parents don't respond well to him or to her being with him. They reassure each other that these are surmountable challenges and that they'll figure it out.

Meanwhile, as our focus shifts to new action and dialogue, we learn that the other cluster of actors are portraying three members of the girl's family, seated at a table perhaps having finished a meal. Her mom and dad and her sister—who is obviously a college student—are talking, first about how things are going, whether or not her boyfriend is coming home with her for the next holiday, how much they all like him, and how intriguing it is to imagine them building a life together.

The father is the primary speaker and he has physical mannerisms and an affectation in his speech that lets the audience know this is a family of privilege and wealth. However, he is also (unintentionally) hilarious. The comedic element is very much alive here, but it is mitigated a bit by the turn of the conversation toward the fact that her sister is late and probably out with the boy whom her dad dislikes. He says, among other things, "I'm raising my daughter on Fifth Avenue, and she is with some guy from the Bronx."

Our attention shifts back to the couple turning into the driveway and the young man asking his date for the garage door opener which she hands him. They pull into the garage and decide that they are ready to face her parents and let them know that their relationship is serious. But first, they decide to hug and kiss a bit longer.

We return to the dinner table where the sister says, "I think I just heard the garage door," and she gets up to go check. From the garage, she calls to her parents to "come see"…either amused or disturbed by witnessing the intimacy of her sister with her beau…and the parents do come out to see it, as well. At this point, there is an explosion of anger and upset from the parents—primarily the father—and the whole group winds up in the dining area where the parents make their displeasure in the prodigal daughter's behavior and choices clearly known and discount the seriousness of the relationship.

The criticized daughter assertively disagrees with her parents and says that she and her boyfriend love each other and they plan to get married. The father blows up at that point, and escalates his disapproval to the point that the put-upon daughter grabs her boyfriend by the hand and returns to the garage to leave. The rest of the family continues to gripe and grumble, but they begin to settle into the rest of their evening.

The lovers are back in the car where they are clearly shaken, and after some half-hearted reflections of what they just experienced, he asks her if the door is closed, and she says yes. He turns on the ignition, but instead of opening the garage door, they just embrace each other and sit still. It is now clear that they have a disturbing Plan B.

The audience does not know how much time has passed, but we learn that the sister returns to the garage at some point, sees her sister and boyfriend sitting in the car with the motor running and the garage door closed, lets out a blood-curdling scream, and the whole family rushes to the garage to discover their unconscious and lifeless bodies. The last spoken words we hear amidst their frantic action to save them is an urgent, "Call 911!" Then, the actors freeze.

IMITATION OF LIFE

We fully go in this scene from the comic to the tragic before it concludes, and end up dealing with many points of discussion about what we witness, what it means, and why it matters.

And There's More...

You may be thinking that all of the scenes end up heavy and serious. They do not...nor do they have to. You may also notice we have not drifted very far from the dramatic in our discussion so far. But we're not done yet.

For example, to start off one skit, a guy sits down on a stool with a guitar, cowboy hat, and dark glasses, and says, "Brothers and sisters, consider what your life would be like...if everything out of your mouth...was the truth." I wish I could tell you exactly what happens next, but that's precisely where the videotape I was watching ends, and my memory of what happened twenty-five years ago (in this case) is just a little fuzzy!

But let's consider the possibilities presented by speculation or imagination:

- The guy could launch into one or more songs, and it could be any one of these:
    - What Is Truth? – Johnny Cash
    - Gimme Some Truth – John Lennon
    - Policy of Truth – Depeche Mode
    - Truth and Honesty – Aretha Franklin
    - The Eyes of Truth – Enigma
    - Truth Hurts – Deep Purple
    - Don't Tell A Lie About Me – James Brown
    - More?
- The guitar could offer a musical soundtrack to action that takes place in a scene that follows...or it could *be* the scene. If it *is* a musical soundtrack source, it could be the two-note

Jaws theme, or a lullaby, a loping cowboy song, or something with Mexican flair, or some other mood setting music.
- The scene might be about truth being delivered without tact or diplomacy, hurting the feelings of others.
- The scene might be about the consequences of telling the truth always and how it is ultimately better than lying.
- The scene might be about trust that is gained when someone is known as a very honest person.
- The scene might show a "rewind" where one or more characters start off telling lies and reap certain outcomes, then they get a "do over," make truthful choices, and have very different consequences occur.

The possibilities are endless, and the guitar and one or more singers could be integral to the unfolding of the presentation at every step...or not. The message could be like that of Depeche Mode and emphasize...

> **You'll see your problems multiplied**
> **If you continually decide**
> **To faithfully pursue**
> **The policy of truth.**

...or it might be more like Johnny Cash singing...

> **This old world's wakin' to a new born day,**
> **And I solemnly swear that it'll be their way.**
> **You better help the voice of youth find**
> **"What is truth?"**

Syd Barrett, the original front man for Pink Floyd, once said, "I think it's good if a song has more than one meaning. Maybe that kind of song can reach far more people."

Maybe it's also true that the meaning you want to convey can be done with more than one song, or you can reach people's minds by having them dismantle a straw dog argument (in a song or otherwise) for that express purpose—so they can discuss its disadvantages and offer different and better ideas.

Sometimes instrumental music is all you need to invoke a feeling that would be hard to create in any other way. Consider, for example, the familiarity of the hymn "Amazing Grace." If someone plays the melody on a flute, bagpipes, guitar, or accordion, or simply hums the tune, it can create an instant mood for many people. Or what about "Here Comes the Bride" by Richard Wagner, or the first six notes of the main melody of Mendelsohn's "Bridal March," or Taps, or "America the Beautiful," or "God Bless America," or the "ABC Song," or even "Mary Had a Little Lamb," or "Twinkle, Twinkle, Little Star?" All of these and many more call particular thoughts, feelings, memories, and moods to mind for many people.

Then there's dance.

America's Hopi tribe asserts, "To watch us dance is to hear our hearts speak." Choreographer Mia Michaels, who is a well-known judge on the TV show, "So You Think You Can Dance," has said, "Dancing is a feeling expressed from the inside out." Well, that much is clear for anyone who sees dance beautifully expressed.

And speaking of beautifully expressed dance, not many were as exciting to watch than Michael Jackson. The late King of Pop once said, "I love the whole world of dance, because dancing is really the emotions through bodily movement. And however you feel, you just bring out the inner feeling through your mood…people don't think about the importance of it."

I have seen an amazing improv from a high school group from Tooele, Utah where all the performers came out with their backs turned to the audience and donned masks that mimicked mime white face. In their presentation, not a single word was spoken. Everything expressed was in mime and dance…and the meanings could not have been clearer.

Last, let's touch on the visual art element of improv.

First of all, it is astounding what you can do with signs and symbols and letters and numbers—displayed, carried, or worn. It doesn't matter if they are hastily sketched, or carefully painted. Secondly, it is amazing what you can do with the right prop or costume piece, from the simple to the sublime. Third, it is intriguing to note how much of a difference you can make in a scene with wooden boxes, chairs, tables, ladders, or even brooms or mops, buckets or stools, or pieces of lattice work, and so much more.

Ultimately, the impact of all levels of visual art employed in creative theater was expressed beautifully by Confucius more than 5,000 years ago: "A picture is worth a thousand words."

With Improv, We Teach and We Learn

Musician Phil Collins said, "In learning you will teach, and in teaching you will learn."

Improvisational theater will rarely be performed on sophisticated sets like the ones you might see in a play or musical…and there is no need for it to be. But when artfully applied in simple but effective and colorful ways, drama, music, dance, and visual artistry can move an audience to tears, laughter, thought, and positive change. This would be enough. And yet, the benefits to the performers are also amazing. But don't take *my* word for it, or the word of Phil Collins. Instead consider the words of two former American Secretaries of Education:

> "The arts are an essential element of education, just like reading, writing, And arithmetic…music, dance, painting, and theater are all keys that unlock profound human understanding and accomplishment."
>
> —William Bennett, Former U.S. Secretary of Education

> "I believe arts education in music, theater, dance, and the visual arts is one of the most creative ways we have to find the gold that is buried just beneath the surface. They (children) have an enthusiasm for life a spark of creativity, and vivid imaginations that need training—training that prepares them to become confident young men and women."
>
> —Richard W. Riley, Former U.S. Secretary of Education

Former President Barack Obama once said, "The future belongs to young people with an education and the imagination to create." Indeed. Give them opportunities for both through improv flavored by all the arts imaginable. And if you think it's all fluff and doesn't matter in the "real world," consider these assertions:

> "We need people who think with the creative side of their brains—people who have played in a band, who have painted…it enhances symbiotic thinking capabilities, not always thinking in the same paradigm, learning how to kick-start a new idea, or how to get a job done better, less expensively."
>
> —Annette Byrd, GlaxoSmithKline

> "A broad education in the arts helps give children a better understanding of their world…We need students who are culturally literate as well as math and science literate."
>
> —Paul Ostergard, Vice President, Citicorp

"Arts education aids students in skills needed in the workplace: flexibility, the ability to solve problems and communicate, the ability to learn new skills, to be creative and innovative, and to strive for excellence."

—Joseph M. Calahan, Director of Cooperate Communications, Xerox Corporation

Enough said?

"Oh, Great Spirit, grant that I not criticize my brother
until I have walked two weeks in his moccasins."
—Edwin Laughing Fox

"One person's craziness is another person's reality."
—Tim Burton

"Some people see the glass half full. Others see it half empty.
I see a glass that's twice as big as it needs to be."
—George Carlin

"There are no facts, only interpretations."
—Friedrich Nietzsche

"In common use, almost every word has many shades of meaning,
and therefore needs to be interpreted by the context."
—Alfred Marshall

"Most misunderstandings in the world could be avoided if people
would simply take the time to ask, "What else could this mean?"
—Shannon L. Alder

CHAPTER 7

Processing

Benjamin Franklin is quoted as saying, "Tell me and I forget, teach me and I may remember, involve me and I learn." What makes the magic with processing is that people are <u>involved</u> in the performance…and more likely to learn.

How many times have you seen a good movie, a play or musical, and enjoyed the conversation afterward maybe as much as actually seeing the show? And if the show wasn't very good, the conversation might even be better than what you witnessed. Either way, the conversation matters.

Now imagine that the conversation is part of the experience—not something that just happens, but by design. This is the model we inherit. This is improvisational theater married to processing…like salt and pepper, sugar and cream, bacon and eggs, hand and glove. It is about the performance, but it is also about its significance…and it is not left to chance, nor is it left to a single interpretation.

And consider this: When you experience a story for the first time, and it is a really, really puzzling mystery, in which you can't figure out "whodunit' for a long time…if ever…and maybe you are surprised at the end because of a twist you couldn't see coming, the possibilities along the way may be many and varied. You might make an assertion to other audience members, or ask a question about something that was said or done that you misunderstood or misinterpreted. And little by little, the clues come together for one or more of the folks who witnessed the story, and you either get it...or you don't. And sometimes...when the story is all over, you *still* walk out with questions in your mind or doubts or troubles, or hope and expectation in your heart.

Life, itself, is often just that way—a mystery that can keep you puzzled indefinitely. On the other hand, when you can examine it the way you would a movie, or a play, or an incident on the highway, at a school or church, or in your neighborhood...and then you *talk* about it with your neighbors and friends who may have seen things you didn't, or heard things you missed, or interpreted things in ways you never considered, suddenly your understanding is magnified, and the meaning can become clearer.

What is Processing?

One definition of "processing" in the general lexicon is "movement of data or material towards a known goal or end result, by passing it through a series of stages or a sequence of actions."

According to the business dictionary, process is a "sequence of interdependent and linked procedures which, at every stage, consume one or more resources (employee time, energy, machines, money) to convert inputs (data, material, parts, etc.) into outputs. These outputs then serve as inputs for the next stage until a known goal or end result is reached." These are good definitions, but let me simplify them for you.

In the prototypes we have been examining from trainings called Improvisational Teen Theatre and Imitation of Life, the greatest commonality was not only the processing, but the way it was simplified for easy consumption. The pattern was briefly outlined this way:

What?
SO what?
NOW what?

IMITATION OF LIFE

The fuller version was taught as:

What happened?
SO what does it mean?
NOW what will you do with it?

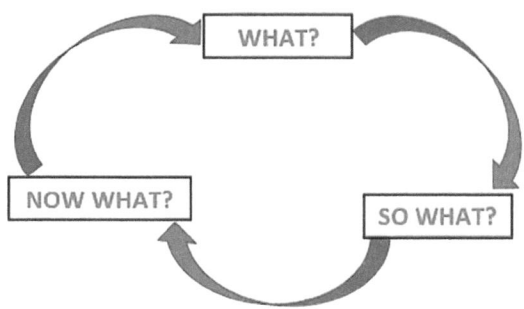

You can find representations of this model in many places, and by different names. It might be called "Kolb's Model of Learning," in which case it would be represented this way:

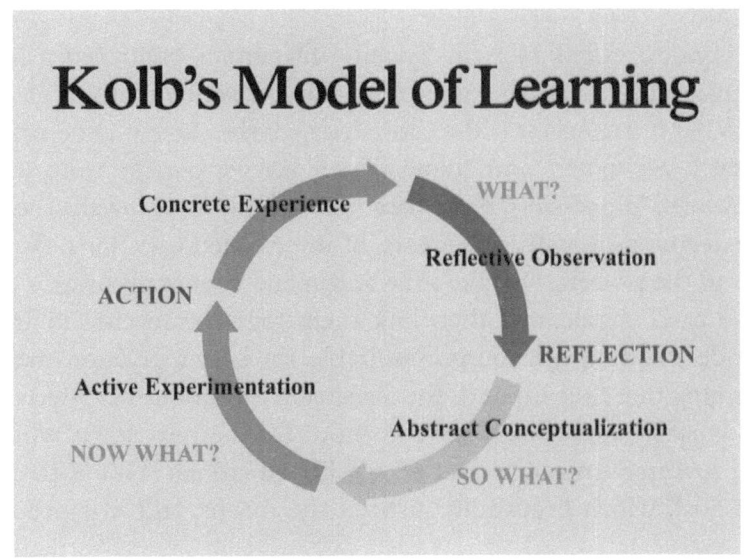

It could be referred to as "the process of reflection" and find expression in this model by Bruce Britton and Olivier Serrat:

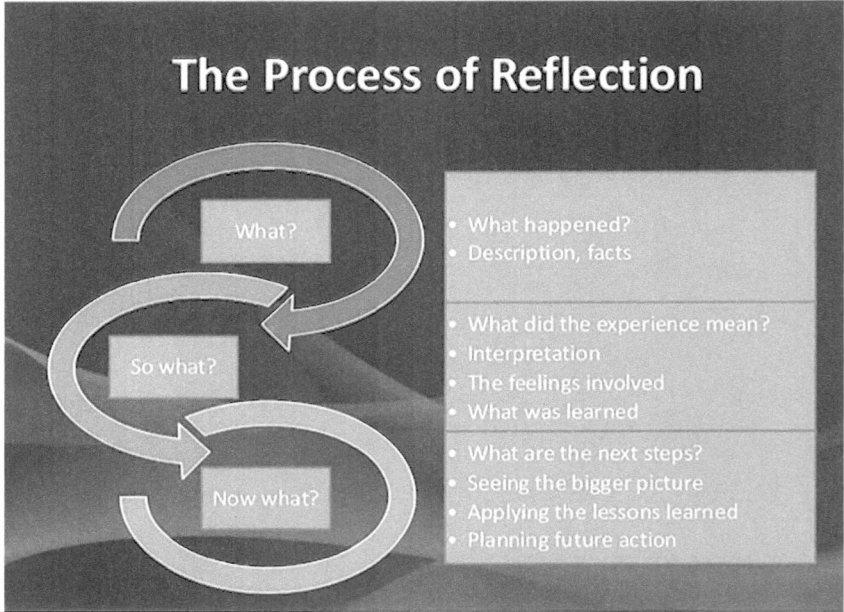

A group called Human Systems Dynamics published a retrospective calling a similar model the "adaptive action method."

What is important is the consistency of the three main elements: "What," "So what?" and "Now what?" As we borrow from earlier definitions, "processing" seeks data that can move us toward the goal of understanding with a sequence of interrelated questions. At each stage in the process, we take time and spend energy gleaning a piece of the total puzzle, and then link them together to convert inputs of understanding into outputs suitable for better decision making. Assuming that the output of the discussion is of the anticipated value, then what is learned *does* serve as input for the next stage, which is more successful management of real life situations. This is the ultimate goal, which beautifully justifies the means, and it is primarily about the questions we ask. As Albert Einstein declared, "It is not that I'm so smart. But I stay with the questions much longer."

Synthesizing a Better Viewpoint

Police officers, detectives, and attorneys routinely report that eye witness accounts are notoriously unreliable. Sometimes a single incident or event observed by ten different people can lead to ten different reports. On other occasions, though, a significant percentage of the observations will dovetail or synchronize in a way that *is* reliable. Out of ten witnesses, six or seven may agree on important details. Even if it is not the same six or seven for each detail, the similarity from one witness to another is useful.

As C.S. Lewis wrote in *The Magician's Nephew*, "What you see and hear depends a good deal on where you are standing: it also depends on what sort of person you are." This is part of the beauty of prioritizing processing as part of a creative theater experience geared toward discovery or edification. "Where you are standing" in this instance represents the point of view informed by your experiences and lessons, and perhaps "the sort of person you are" is mirrored in your insights or convictions about what the experiences meant—or *could* mean, and how you apply them.

On the flip side, however, we can heed Bertrand Russell who reminds us, "In all affairs it's a healthy thing now and then to hang a question mark on the things you have long taken for granted." We should be willing to let go, once in a while, of our sacred cow points of view. It does not have to be uncommon for a perspective to shift by virtue of having been exposed to another that is more useful, accurate, helpful, empowering, or any number of other factors that can be employed for greater understanding or better outcomes.

I am reminded of a story I often tell about a social media exchange I once had with my wife's stepbrother. I don't think he and I are complete polar opposites in terms of our political and philosophical views, but we are much more different in these regards than we are alike. We do have respect for each other, however, and we have engaged in productive dialogue even though we sometimes must agree to disagree. And once in a while, we will start from a place of marked polarity, and after one or the other offers a well-articulated alternate view, the other will say—at least on a point or two here and there—"I agree."

I was the one who shifted on the occasion that sticks out in my mind. It started with me on a bit of a rant (diplomatically, of course). I was railing against the dangers of nuclear power and advocating for alternative energy sources that are safer, more sustainable, and less environmentally impactful. Mike, who is a retired Navy officer of high rank, weighed in afterward with a comment that substantially moderated my point of view.

Basically, he pointed out that the U.S. Navy has many nuclear-powered submarines that have been constantly in operation for dozens of years, and there has never been an incident. He ended his comment by stating that nuclear power, itself, is not so much the problem, but it is a question of scale and management.

I immediately embraced his logic and stood corrected. Though I still have major concerns about disasters like those at Fukushima Daiichi in 2011, Chernobyl in 1986, and Three Mile Island in 1979, I now couch my argument in terms shaped, in significant part, by a single comment from a respected person who arrived at his point of view much differently than I arrived at mine. As the articulate Ms. George Eliot wrote, "It is a narrow mind which cannot look at a subject from various points of view." Never let it be said that I own such a mind.

Not Necessarily Right or Wrong

In *The Beauties of Nature and the Wonders of the World We Live In*, by John Lubbock, he writes, "What we do see depends mainly on what we look for. […] In the same field the farmer will notice the crop, the geologists the fossils, botanists the flowers, artists the colouring, sportsmen the cover for the game. Though we may all look at the same things, it does not all follow that we should see them."

This is why we process creative theatrical scenes. Although we may witness the same scene unfold on stage, we don't all see the same things. We interpret everything through the experiential lenses we look through as we focus our view. It is not that our viewpoints are necessarily right or wrong, but they are incomplete, or biased, limited, or prejudiced, narrow, or blinded, naïve, or immature, unsophisticated, or…yes…mistaken or correct are options, too.

Isaac Asimov in *I, Robot*, wrote, "It is the obvious which is so difficult to see most of the time. People say, 'It's as plain as the nose on your face.' But how much of the nose on your face can you see, unless someone holds a mirror up to you?" This is exactly what creative improvisational theater pieces can do…hold up a mirror of life…an imitation of life…in a way that allows us to see the "obvious" in ways we may not have before.

The end result we can all hope for and work toward is to make people more capable of meeting challenges. It is about learning, about understanding, about meaning. And it is about excellence in all these areas.

It's About Meaning and Excellence

Those of us who are expressive seek to put into words the noteworthy thoughts we have about what life means, and from time to time we succeed admirably. This is why I collect quotes from such people, and why I hope to be one of these quoted people from time to time. Sometimes an insight is expressed so beautifully that we do a disservice to our languages not to adopt the words and expressions that others arrive at before us. In other words, I love a good quote.

In this spirit, we'll end this chapter with a bevy of quotes about meaning and excellence that are nonpareil, and yet delightfully supportive of the end game of scene processing. I'll try not to hurt you with the flood of them, but if I do, I promise that it will hurt so good!

But first, a caveat.

Iconic artist Andy Warhol once said, "I'm afraid that if you look at a thing long enough, it loses all of its meaning." There is such a thing as too much processing, but there is no specific formula for how much is too much. It is the kind of awareness that facilitators must learn to intuitively recognize based on the flow of passionate comments, questions and revelations, as well as body language, facial expressions such as the "eyes glazed over" look, or by recognizing in our audiences when, as my college art history professor used to say, they have reached a "saturation point." (Stay tuned for the story in Chapter 10.)

And how dedicated should we be in our delivery of these experiences? Let's take a tip from Martin Luther King, Jr. "All labor that uplifts humanity has dignity and importance and should be undertaken with painstaking excellence." Provided that the group present is happily engaged in barreling toward empowering outcomes of understanding and expansion, and you have enough shared time, have at it—and focus on excellence in your provision! Here's why. Miguel de Unamuno stated, "Art distills sensations and embodies it with enhanced meaning." Maya Angelou said, "Words mean more than what is set down on paper. It takes the human voice to infuse them with deeper meaning." Distilling sensations and infusing deeper meaning is exactly what happens when ideas are voiced on stage through creative theater.

> "Consciously or not, we are all on a quest for answers, trying to learn the lessons of life. We grapple with fear and guilt. We search for meaning, love, and power. We try to understand fear, loss, and time. We seek to discover who we are and how we can become truly happy." (Elisabeth Kubler-Ross)

> "Change is the end result of all true learning." (Leo Buscaglia)

"For the meaning of life differs from man to man, from day to day and from hour to hour. What matters, therefore, is not the meaning of life in general but rather the specific meaning of a person's life at a given moment." (Viktor E. Frankl)

Or maybe, "Life is without meaning. You bring the meaning to it. The meaning of life is whatever you ascribe it to be. Being alive is the meaning." (Joseph Campbell)

It's all about what we believe, and Tony Robbins says, "Beliefs have the power to create and the power to destroy. Human beings have the awesome ability to take any experience of their lives and create a meaning that disempowers them or one that can literally save their lives."

With the experience of creative theater such as what we are exploring, we can "Be the light that helps others see; it is what gives life its deepest significance," as Roy T. Bennett stated in *The Light in the Heart*.

Also, "Learning never exhausts the mind," (Leonardo Da Vinci) and "True teachers are those who use themselves as bridges over which they invite their students to cross; then, having facilitated their crossing, joyfully collapse, encouraging them to create their own." (Nikos Kazantzakis)

We can be these kinds of teachers and reach students and audiences with improv and other creative theatrics, and we can do so with excellence and a focus on meaning.

"All humans change. Development is our life…
Without change, there's no growth."
—Mimi Kennedy

"When what we introduce into the children's world of ideas and feelings is in line with the direction of the developmental forces of a given stage of life, we strengthen the entire developing person in a way that remains a source of strength throughout that person's life."
—Rudolf Steiner

"There's only one thing harder than living in a home with an adolescent—and that's being an adolescent. The moodiness, the volatility, the wholesale lack of impulse control, all would be close to clinical conditions if they occurred at another point in life. In adolescence, they're just part of the behavioral portfolio."
—Jeffrey Kluger

"Even as kids reach adolescence, they need more than ever for us to watch over them. Adolescence is not about letting go. It's about hanging on during a very bumpy ride."
—Ron Taffel

"Times of transition are strenuous, but I love them. They are an opportunity to purge, rethink priorities, and be intentional about new habits. We can make our new normal any way we want."
—Kristin Armstrong

"A lot of people resist transition and therefore never allow themselves to enjoy who they are. Embrace the change, no matter what it is; once you do, you can learn about the new world you're in and take advantage of it."
—Nikki Giovanni

"We gain strength, and courage, and confidence by each experience in which we really stop to look fear in the face… we must do that which we think we cannot."
—Eleanor Roosevelt

"Give people enough guidance to make the decisions you want them to make. Don't tell them what to do, but encourage them to do what is best."
—Jimmy Johnson

CHAPTER 8

"The Back-To-School Special"

One summer, a close friend called me. She imagined I would be a good candidate to help her and a small group of her friends deal with a troublesome challenge. She was a single mother and her son would be starting the first year of junior high in the fall, and four of her friends were in the exact same parenting situation.

Connie and I became friends when we were both on staff at the same junior high, so she knew me and knew a lot about the way I operated as an educator. The moms had boys, and she thought they all might benefit from a male perspective. She asked if I would put together a little workshop for the mothers and sons collectively, and I happily agreed.

She pulled together the group of them, and we spent several hours exploring the concerns, fears, expectations, and anticipated challenges of moving from the elementary level of education to the beginning of the secondary experience. Afterward, Connie reported back to me that the mothers and their sons all felt like the discussion was helpful and that they had a clearer sense of what to expect. It was a good experiment.

What if...

Now, fast forward a year or so.

Connie came over for a visit one day, and as she chatted with me and my wife, she told us about something that was on her mind. She launched into a brief monologue and said something like, "You know, I've been thinking...You remember that workshop you did for me and my friends? If that kind of workshop was good for us, it would also be good for other parents and kids going through the same experience. What if we put together something that we could present? Maybe we could do a show, and then a question and answer period afterward."

The idea was immediately intriguing. Between the three of us, we had what seemed like just the right mix of skills and talents. We were all educators with involvement at the elementary or middle level of education. We all had experiences and competencies related to the theater. We could all write, sing, and dance a little. We understood a lot about the particular challenges presented to families when their children start emerging into adolescence—including heightened peer influences, increased expectations of responsibility, and the need for increasing academic prowess presented in the post-elementary school world. We were also at the right ages ourselves in order to relate well to both parents and kids.

We started brainstorming possibilities and making notes and outlines. In a relatively short time, we had an idea of what such an experience would look like. We imagined a mini-musical with songs and skits, which would unfold in about an hour and demonstrate things that middle school kids and their parents could expect. Examples included lockers and locker combinations, a team of teachers to respond to instead of just one or two, a much larger building, bullies, fears, choices, overwhelm, girlfriends and boyfriends, parties and temptations, and more.

We could see the show reflecting many of these challenges to some degree, as well as ways to manage them. We also talked about offering refreshments and another half hour or so afterward for parents and kids to ask questions and address any remaining concerns with us and each other. It just all made sense and seemed possible, but we had no idea (if we put it all together) whether schools would be interested in investing in its potential. We knew how to find out, however.

We immediately got on the telephone and called a handful of junior high principals we knew…and asked. They all said that if we held this event, they could see the value of investing in it. So, we went to work. A couple of months later, by the time school was in session again in the fall, we had a pilot of what we called "The Back-To-School Special" with music and vignettes that we had written, rehearsed, and for which we had created musical soundtracks, *and* we were booked for our first shows. The only thing left to do was to stand and deliver, and see if families agreed about the value. They did. The show was a hit.

Within the first six to eight weeks of the new semester, we took the stage eight times at eight different schools, and spent a couple of hours entertaining and educating appreciative audiences of parents and children who were beginning this important transitional time for youngsters entering a new level of school life. They had an opportunity to begin to more fully imagine some of the trials, and to put their minds together with others to consider how they would manage.

So, would you like to take a peek at what we did? Prepare your imagination and let's take a look at the kind of experience we created for parents and kids to share together. It was a lot of fun, and at times a little emotional, too.

"The Back-To-School Special"

We opened the show with a song called "I'm Going Crazy," which probably summed up what some members of the families in our audiences were feeling. We quickly touched on everything from larger buildings, fashion challenges, zits and other embarrassments, to separation anxiety, drug pushers, perverts, refusal skills, expectations and the illusion of control for the parents. With that as the backdrop, we launched into a scene that featured a boy waking up from a nightmare yelling, and then being comforted by his mother who comes to the rescue. Here is the opening section of the script:

> Boy: *(From sleep, and out of a nightmare)* Help! Help! Dad! DAD! It's gonna get me!
> Mom: *(Entering as if from another room)* What's gonna get you? What's the matter, baby?
> Boy: Mom...where's Dad?! I think this is a job for the MAN!
> Mom: Well, "The MAN" isn't back from Chicago yet, so it's just me and you kid! Now what's the matter?
> Boy: What's the matter??!! This big...fat...UGLY monster was trying to eat me alive right down the hall from the gym at school! That's what's the matter! So what are you gonna do about it?
> Mom: Nothing. It was just a nightmare, honey. Go back to sleep!
> Boy: Unh-unh!!! That funky breath crawling up my nose and that grease drippin' all over me was not a dream! Look at all this grease all over my bed!
> Mom: That's sweat all over your bed and if you didn't brush your teeth after the onion rings you ate tonight, that would explain the breath. (Fanning her nose) Whew! You better believe that will explain it!
> Boy: Mom! Give me a break! That was scary!
> Mom: I'm not surprised, honey. Being in middle school can be pretty frightening. But you will handle it. Don't worry about it.
> Boy: Don't worry about it! That's like saying don't worry about Billy Jones! Everybody <u>knows</u> he's the meanest dude at school! Come to think of it, the monster kinda looked like Billy.
> Mom: And he probably looked like he had a locker on his body for armor too, didn't he?
> Boy: *(Surprised)* How did you know THAT?
> Mom: Because you've been complaining about your locker ever since school started.

From this point, mother and son talk about locker combinations, the "seriously hot" girl he likes, Mom's inside information about a girl she knows about who secretly likes *him*, and the fact that she and his dad know a little something about what he's going through from their own experiences (which he slights, of course, albeit playfully). Before she heads back to bed, she leaves him with a message in which she says, in part:

> **Sometimes the new experiences we encounter in life can seem to be really overwhelming when we first see them [but you] know secrets you don't even know you know yet. And the more you know, the more you will find out that you can handle all kinds of monsters…even the ones that look like Billy Jones with a locker on his head.**

The boy then says to himself, shortly after Mom leaves, "You don't scare me, big, fat monster!" And from there, we launch into our second song (and dance) to an upbeat tune we initially called "Big, Fat Monster." Later, we decided it was more developmentally appropriate to switch the term "Dream Invader" for "Big, Fat Monster," but otherwise the song remained unchanged. *(The lyrics appear at the end of this chapter)*.

Part of our formula in creating this show was to make it as relevant and accessible as possible. We performed it ourselves for two seasons following up the eight-show debut with a thirteen-show sophomore season the following year. By then, we were already envisioning making the vehicle available to schools as a packaged product that they could produce using student performers. The idea was to soon have ninth grade students perform the show for incoming seventh graders—or eighth grade students for new sixth graders as the case may have been for some schools.

Meanwhile, we were moving toward creating a new show called "Masters of the Hormones" that we knew would draw interest, as well. That is, as long as we could find a way to approach it that would not cause parental alarm due to dealing with issues related to sexuality. But that is another story, and there is more to this one.

A hip fairy godmother showed up for a pre-teen female character, and a song was presented called "Life is Choices" followed by a brief lesson on decision-making. Then there was a funky piece called "The Inappropriate Rap," which very appropriately talked about all the things that were *not* appropriate for kids to be doing, thinking, saying, etc. For example:

> **Reckless thinkin' can take a life!**
> **Why put yourself through all that strife?**
> **Drinkin' alcohol just ain't cool!**
> **It doesn't work when you go to school.**
> **Shoplifting has a heavy price.**
> **If you plan to steal, you better think twice!**
> **Don't tear up someone's property!**
> **It's not your stuff, so let it be!**
> **Cigarette smoke can make you choke**
> **And make you broke. That ain't no joke!**
> **Doing drugs can get you high,**
> **Or lay you low if you should die.**

We brought kids on stage to role play refusal skills after the rap, and engaged the audience in reciting a related litany next. Another piece on making decisions followed, after which we had parents and children work together in dyads on a model focused on using declarative language, and working for cooperative win-win solutions to contentious issues.

Then, after presenting an outline on goal-setting, and singing a song called "I'm Not Going Crazy Anymore," we shared a brief summary of all the concepts, and invited our guests to stay for the after-show party/discussion immediately following. Then we took a quick break while our host school broke out the refreshments, and returned to sit on the edge of the stage (or hang out in some other location) where we could take questions and address concerns while the families enjoyed their snacks and drinks…and completed simple evaluation forms for us, which was primary to our quality control strategy.

It was important for us to know for sure whether we were delivering as promised with our show. In the cover letter that went out to schools with our other marketing materials, we promised this, among other outcomes:

> **The Back-to-School Special is an assembly-type program which focuses attention on the potential concerns of what is generally one of the most at-risk groups in our schools—students in transition. But it also offers strategies for understanding and dealing with those concerns that are appropriate for students, parents, and educators. The program is designed to be presented in a 75-minute evening and features theatrical, musical, experiential, and didactic elements. We think you will be interested in this unique way of addressing some of the issues peculiar to students—and parents—who are involved in secondary school transition.**

The evaluations gave us just the feedback we needed to keep on track with delivering what families really needed, and what *we* needed in order to feel we were adding value.

These are a few of the hundreds of comments people shared with us:

> *"I wish my son in 9th grade would have had this program. It was great."*

> *"Give copies of words so [we] can take [them] home esp. 'Fairy Godmother and 'Refusal Skills Rap.'"*

> *"It was great and down to the real thing. Thanks."*

"Especially enjoyed the 'One-on-One' discussions. 'Big Fat Monster' [is a] great song. Granny was great!"

"Excellent! You addressed all those fears and insecurities that I remember so well and that I see my daughter struggling with today. I could see her reaction, 'How did they know!?'"

"This production was excellent. All summer my son worried about junior high. This might be an excellent program for them to see at the end of sixth grade. Hope you continue with it."

"Excellent—lots of food for thought. Do you do programs other than for [the] school system? (Like for nurses?)"

"I saw both parents and children responding to the program and I'm not surprised. I did, too, and I'm just an interested friend and teacher from [elsewhere.]"

And to keep us humble and improving:

"Some of the songs were a little too long…"

"Great, but may in certain ways be embarrassing to some kids."

"Presentation would be easier to see if on a stage…"

"Room too small. Program too long—cut out 'Granny.'"

"Middle of program mentioned 'Fight for what you believe in.' The phrase was repeated. I think the words 'take a stand for what you believe in' prevents any children from thinking [about] a physical fight."

Why This Program Mattered...and Worked

This last sample comment is indicative of the level of concern parents are capable of entertaining when their children are beginning to mature and face the broad challenges of life as an adolescent. As Academy Award-winning film and television producer Edward Zwick has said, "Adolescence is a time in which you experience everything more intensely." Well, *that's* for sure, and it often goes for the parents, too.

Writer Harlan Coben asserted, "Make no mistake, adolescence is a war. No one gets out unscathed." Of course, you might expect a comment like this from a guy who writes mystery novels and thrillers that often feature murders, fatal accidents and plot twists galore. And yet, he is not far from the truth when you consider adolescents sometimes go from friendships that happen by default to feeling as if they have no friends and it's *their* fault. They are caught up in a swirl of internal and external pressures that can leave them feeling helpless and hopeless. But as Phil Schiller, the senior vice president of worldwide marketing at Apple, said, "There's a little bit of pain in every transition, but we can't let that stop us from making it. If we did, we'd never make any progress at all."

The key to success for families is to work on emerging into this period of trial with as much insight about what to expect as possible. This is where an opportunity like those presented by imitating life through theater can come in quite handy. It gives folks a chance to peek into the good, the bad and the ugly of the world into which they are entering, and perhaps better prepare.

Iconic educator Maria Montessori describes some of the confusions of this kind of transitional period in these terms: "The chief symptom of adolescence is a state of expectation, a tendency towards creative work, and a need for the strengthening of self-confidence. Suddenly, the child becomes very sensitive to the rudeness and humiliations which he had previously suffered with patient indifference." But wait a minute—this is exactly why IOL works as well as it does!

Adolescence is a state of expectation? Absolutely! Families going through it together have all kinds of expectations, both positive and negative. Adolescents have a tendency toward creative work? Well, duh! Turn 'em loose to work creatively on addressing the things that concern and trouble them. There is a need for the strengthening of self-confidence? IOL *does* that for both performers *and* audience members. Check! And if it's true they become very sensitive to rudeness and humiliation which they had previously suffered through as if it didn't really matter, they can begin to more fully awaken to the fact that it *does* matter, but they do it from places of empowerment and empathy rather than with helplessness or insensitivity.

And don't think the above-average parent necessarily has any edge on the garden variety mom or dad. Alison Gopnik is a developmental psychologist, but she says being one "didn't make me any better at dealing with my own children, no. I muddled through, and, believe me, fretted and worried with the best of them."

Original "Little Shop of Horrors" star, Ellen Greene, stated, "It's a very hard thing for all of us to accept ourselves at all the different stages—the horrible side, the wonderful side, the adorable side—and who you are as a grownup. And then to bring what you learned as a child to that grownup: that is the magic of creativity." And this is exactly the kind of creativity we take advantage of with creative and relevant theater like what we are discussing here.

"Making good decisions is a crucial skill at every level," said highly respected management consultant, Peter Drucker. Really? Then let's give our kids some practice, even if it's by proxy, and while they can experiment safely with the possibilities.

As journalist Laura Addison wrote in the Wichita Eagle-Beacon newspaper when the Back-to-School Special opened, "Preteens have heard it all before. Don't drink. Don't smoke. Don't do drugs or have sex. But how can you tell them again, and be sure you're being heard? You *might* try three dudes in shades and fedoras doing the 'Inappropriate Behavior Rap.'"

Yeah, you might…or any number of other creative strategies that hold promise for getting and keeping the attention of the folks you want to impact from the stage.

Can you see it yet?

BIG, FAT MONSTER

Words by - Robert Simon Music by - Robert Simon

Verse 1. You don't scare me, big, fat monster!
    I can knock you down to size!
    At the time that I first saw you,
    I could not believe my eyes!
    But when I looked at you closer,
    I could see you were nothing
    at all! (You faker!)

Verse 2. I at first thought you were awesome
    When I did not understand;
    But I know now you're a turkey,
    And I'm gonna take a stand!
    Since I've seen through your disguises,
    You should know you don't scare
    me at all! (You turkey!)

Chorus: I believe you were only in my mind,
Bridge: And I can think you out!
    Other victims you're gonna have to find,
    'Cause I have too much clout!
        You're no cause for alarm;
        And you can't do anyone harm.
        And in case there's something
        you've missed,
            It's this simple: You just
            do not exist!

Verse 3. You don't scare me, big, fat monster!
　　　　　I know secrets you don't know!
　　　　　I am sure I have the courage
　　　　　To stand with you—toe to toe!
　　　　　And I think it's kind of funny
　　　　　That you think you can scare
　　　　　me at all! (You're silly!)

Verse 4. I won't listen to the people
　　　　　That think I can never win.
　　　　　And if they think you're a monster,
　　　　　I'll say they should think again!
　　　　　'Cause I know you're just illusion!
　　　　　I can see you are nothing at
　　　　　all! (You dreamer!)

Chorus: I believe you were only in my mind,
Bridge: And I can think you out!
　　　　　Other victims you're gonna have to find,
　　　　　'Cause I have too much clout!
　　　　　　　You're no cause for alarm;
　　　　　　　And you can't do anyone harm.
　　　　　　　And in case there's something
　　　　　　　you've missed,
　　　　　　　　　It's this simple: You just
　　　　　　　　　do not exist!

Repeat Verses 1 & 2...

End: You don't scare me, big, fat monster! You don't scare me, big, fat monster!
You don't scare me, big, fat monster!

© 1987 Positive Rhythm Music

"One of the great cosmic laws, I think, is that whatever we hold in our
thought will come true in our experience. When we hold something,
anything, in our thought, then somehow coincidence leads us
in the direction that we've been wishing to lead ourselves."
—Richard Bach

"Coincidence is important, the convergence of different ideas."
—Dries van Noten

"History is for human self-knowledge…the only clue
to what man can do is what man has done."
—R.G. Collingwood

"Art is an effort to create, beside the real world, a more humane world."
—Andre Maurois, French Author

"The first step to controlling your world is to control your culture. To
model and demonstrate the kind of world you demand to live in. to
write the books. Make the music. Shoot the films. Paint the art."
—Chuck Palahniuk, American Novelist and Journalist

"If art is to nourish the roots of our culture, society must set
the artist free to follow his vision wherever it takes him."
—John F. Kennedy, former American President

CHAPTER 9

The Wichita Griots Cultural Arts Camp

The Griots Storytelling Institute was created in 1998 and received nonprofit status in October of 2003. The Griots are dedicated to providing educational storytelling arts in the inner city and the total community. The group partners with other arts and cultural organizations, and youth and community members to develop arts programs using character education stories to teach respect, responsibility, integrity, caring, self-discipline, and more.

The Griots are committed to keeping the oral tradition of the ancient art form of storytelling alive. The goal is to use art to teach literacy, while inspiring and enabling all youth, especially those from disadvantaged circumstances, to realize their full potential as productive, responsible, and caring citizens. They seek to strengthen education, preserve and renew the world's fading cultures, and build peace and understanding among all people...focusing on youth in conflict.

You can read all of this on the Institute's website, but I know it because I am part of it. I also know the group is grounded in Wichita's African-American community, but their programming is available to and experienced by all. Here, however, we will focus on the flagship program of the Griots...the Cultural Arts Camp.

With this particular project, there are goals that include these:

- Offer unique stories about African-American history, its heroes and heroines, and African folktales that might otherwise go unheard
- Promote cultural diversity through storytelling and literature
- Encourage and enhance a desire in children to become or continue as readers
- Provide opportunities for young people to learn and practice cultural arts related skills and talents to improve their sense of self-worth and to entertain and educate an audience
- Seek to demonstrate how the arts can play a role in building bridges of understanding in the community
- Break down barriers, real or imagined, between ethnic groups
- Educate the masses about the historical contributions and accomplishments of African-Americans
- Help African-American children connect to their own rich heritage
- Develop appreciative and creative listening and learning for all

These are all admirable aims, but there is, however, one very specific primary goal: **"to produce a fun and successful cultural arts summer camp experience for 75-100 children age 6-16 and a successful culminating themed stage performance with participants."** The Griots have accomplished this goal, now, for fourteen consecutive summers. Let's see if we can offer evidence from camp history which fulfilled the list of goals expressed above.

But first, a bit of a footnote.

A significant reason the Griots adopted this specific goal as a primary one for the cultural arts camp is because people connected with the Griots also had a connection with the Performing Arts component of the Upward Bound program years before! When the founding group engaged in brainstorming about possibilities, this particular outcome easily bubbled to the top because of memories of both participating in creative theater projects like the ones we are exploring, or witnessing the impact of them on audiences and participants.

But now, let's do some sampling.

1. Offer unique stories about African-American history, its heroes and heroines…

In July of 2016, the camp show was called "The African-American Story: From Chains To Wings," and was a precursor to the arrival of the 35th Annual Conference of the National Association of Black Storytellers…in Wichita…in 2017…for the first time in the organization's history. The theme for the conference would be the same.

The show's script called for scenes that literally took the audience from loading Africans on slave ships for the journey to America to the first pilots of African descent. Chains to wings. Along the way, there were significant treatments of scenes featuring important historical figures including Harriet Tubman, Sojourner Truth, and Frederick Douglas. These were almost obligatory. But have you ever heard of Robert Smalls, Harriet Jacobs, William Harvey Carney, Henry "Box" Brown, or William and Ellen Craft? I imagine not. And yet, they were all able to escape from slavery in determined and creative ways.

Similarly, you may have heard of George Washington Carver, Madame C.J. Walker, Bill "Bojangles" Robinson, and maybe Oscar Micheaux, but it is not likely that you know about Hiram Revels or Blanche Bruce who both served in the U.S. Senate after the Civil War, or early black pilots like Eugene Bullard and Hubert Julian. I would also guess it is a safe bet that you have never heard of Willa Brown, Janet Bragg, or Dorothy Layne McIntyre…all of whom were black *female* pilots *before* Jill Brown Hiltz became the first black woman to serve as a commercial airline pilot in 1978.

And the show was able to introduce so many more unique African American heroes and heroines from macro history beyond. For the first time in the history of the Wichita Griots, the show also consisted of a multi-media presentation that included video and slides.

2. …and African folktales that might otherwise go unheard.

July of 2008 featured a show called "Catchafire," and the title was intentionally a double entendre. The opening narration explained it this way:

> **Catchafire. What does that mean? Well, it depends.**
>
> **If it's two words, it means "start to burn." If it's three words, it means, "to get fire from someone or something else"—like catching a cold or catching a ball.**
>
> **And if it's sort of one word…like it is for us…it means both: start to burn and catch a fire from someone or something else. Either way…or both ways.**
>
> **But then…we need to talk about what the fire is. Because we certainly don't mean the stuff that turns things into ashes.**
>
> **No. For us, the fire is enthusiasm, inspiration, energy, excitement motivation, stimulation, bright ideas, or just plain old interest or concern.**

Folktales from the 2008 show included "The Pot That Juan Built," "The Clever Trickster, Anansi," "Wheels on the Bus," "Kantchil Waits for the World to End," "Drakes Tale," "The Boy Who Cried Wolf," "The Phoenix," and more. These stories were not all from Africa, of course, but they were all folk tales…and tied right into the next goal:

3. **Promote cultural diversity through storytelling and literature [and] break down barriers, real or imagined, between ethnic groups…**

In 2009, the show was called "The Caribbean Connection" and opened with this speech:

> From the beginning of time until 1493, America was inhabited by a great variety of native peoples... and they numbered many thousands if not millions. There is much debate about the world of Native America before Columbus because of a lack of hard evidence. But there are some things that are not debated, and in our exploration of the Caribbean Connection...and especially the *music*, this is one of them.
>
> From the beginning of time until the year 1492, the islands of the Caribbean were inhabited by five native Indian tribes...they were the Arawak, Carib, Cibony, Igneri and Taino, and they had a rhythm that sounded like this!

As you might imagine, there was a hand-drumming demonstration that came right after this speech...and this was just the beginning! Soon to follow were reflections of many connections between natives, Africans, indentured servants from India, and Europeans, and influences that came from these unions of individuals and cultures that included iconic music, dance, and even African religions such as voodoo, Rastafarianism, Shango, and Santeria—to name a few—and superstitions about which some of the youngest performers were *happy* to tell the audience!

4. **Encourage and enhance a desire in children to become or continue as readers.**

The summer show in 2012 was called "R.E.A.D." and it stood for "Read, Empower, And Discover." This show was *all* about reading, and it was also a lot of fun. Here, for example, is the opening scene of the show:

Scene 1 – "PECTOPAH"

(Scene opens with many performers crossing stage, milling around as if sightseeing until stage clears and the following three performers are left, the Bystander seated and reading DSR, the two Kids looking at a sign (PECTOPAH) approximately in the middle of the stage.)

>Kid 1: What the heck does PECK-toe-pah mean?
>Kid 2: I don't know.
>Kid 1: I have never heard of that before.
>Bystander: Actually, you have.
>Kid 1: Huh? What do you mean?
>Bystander: Well, first of all, it doesn't say PECK-toe-pah.
>Kid 2: Well, that's what it looks like.
>Bystander: That's only because you are used to the English Alphabet. That word is based on the Cyrillic alphabet.
>Kid 1: The silly WHAT?
>Bystander: Seh-RILL-ic…C-y-r-i-l-l-i-c. It is the alphabet used in various languages spoken and written in Eastern Europe and Asia, including those spoken in and influenced by Russia.
>Kid 1: So, what does it say?
>Kid 2: Yeah, what does it say?
>Bystander: You tell me. Look at it again and imagine that the letters that look like a "P" actually sound like an "R"…because they do in Russia, for example. Then imagine that the letter you would call a "C" actually sounds like an "S" in that spot. And what looks like an "H?" That's supposed to sound like an "N"…"N" as in Nancy. So now you tell ME what it says!

(The kids work at making the translations out loud. Then…)

>Kid 2: *(Tentatively, not sure)* Re-STOR-an?
>Bystander: Look at the picture.
>Kid 1: *(After a few more moments of puzzling it out, excitedly)* REST-o-ran! It's a RESTAURANT!!!

IMITATION OF LIFE

Bystander: Good job!
Kid 1: *(Proudly)* Thank you!!!
Kid 2: Man! Just when you think you've got reading all figured out, it throws you a curve ball! Cyrillic alphabet. Who KNEW?
Kid 1: *(As they are walking away, they are joined by singers QUIETLY moving in for the following song)* Yeah…and you know what else? This must be what it feels like to people who can't read. It's like everything spelled out in words and letters is a language you can't understand.
Kid 2: You know…I think you're right…

So far, I haven't mentioned much about songs in the shows, but there is always a variety of music. In this show, for instance, songs included "Signs" by the 5 Man Electrical Band, "Library Cheer," a rap by Garrison Keillor, "Get Up" by gospel artists Mary, Mary, and "Education is the Key" by Sweet Honey in the Rock.

This show also featured a story told about Sequoyah, who created a written language for the Cherokees…so yet another example of the multicultural approach to Griot Camp shows.

Also in this show was a feature untried before in any of the previous shows. The final scene was an improv where two of the older actors actually worked from a script outline and created the scene by interacting with the audience around the theme of reading symbols as part of how we read and create meaning.

5. **Seek to demonstrate how the arts can play a role in building bridges of understanding in the community.**

"The Peaceful Warrior" was the title and theme in 2014, but the show opened with a fight. It was in slow motion and gave a few kids the opportunity to practice stage combat. Of course, no one was hurt, but it was the perfect set-up for the opening.

Inspired in part by Dan Millman's book, *The Peaceful Warrior*, the narrators at the beginning of the show acknowledged his writing by name. After the "fight" was over, this is what happened next:

Peaceful Warrior Narration 1

Narrator 1: Did you see that? Raise your hand if you've seen this kind of thing before. It's classic, isn't it? The moment we have a problem with another person, we want to go to war with them—whether it's a war of words, or coming to blows.

Why IS that? And how can we ever achieve peace if our first impulse (so to speak) is to go to war with each other when things go wrong?

Narrator 2: And what about all the people who maybe don't choose violence in their behavior, but they seem to celebrate when others make the choice to be violent? Maybe the people who are "The Audience" are as bad as the ones who swing fists, and shoot guns, and detonate bombs.

Narrator 3: It certainly doesn't help to do nothing, though. As the Irish philosopher, Edmund Burke is reported to have said, **"All that is necessary for the triumph of evil is that good men do nothing."** Of course, he meant women, too. But what do we DO? Well…the answer may be easier than we think. What if more of us became peaceful warriors?

Narrator 4: We know.

Your brain just gets all twisted up when we put peace and war together in the same term. But that's probably because you either have too little imagination, or you don't know your history well enough.

Think we're kidding? Uhhhhhhhhh………we're not. And here's an example. Author, Dan Millman created a story (among others) called Secret of the Peaceful Warrior. See if you can understand from our retelling how a warrior can be peaceful. All you have to do is watch what Danny does when he's the new kid at school and gets targeted by…yeah, you guessed it…the local bully.

And then, of course, there was another scene...after a drum break.

This is another element I have not emphasized for you so far, but children who attend our camp learn hand percussion and particularly drumming. Over the years, it has been mostly African inspired rhythms, but lately many of the Latin and island rhythms have started to creep into the mix with our percussionists who teach, also.

6. **Provide opportunities for young people to learn and practice cultural arts related skills and talents to improve their sense of self-worth and to entertain and educate an audience.**

Perhaps we can use this same show for an example which touches a bit on the above goal.

We invoked a scene from a Karate Kid movie, which we used to segue from the Millman story we told about Danny getting bullied and how he learned to manage that from his mentor, Socrates, to a song. This was the shape it took:

Narration 2

Narrator: We know some of you are thinking, "That's not how it works. Some people just want to <u>fight</u>!" Yes...and some people really <u>don't</u> want to fight. So remember how Socrates answered Danny's question. There are ways to get off the tracks.

I saw Mr. Miyagi do the same thing in a Karate Kid movie once...

(Note: The following bracketed narration/dialogue is optional pending whether a video clip can be shown or not.)

[Narrator: A crazy martial artist wanted to attack him after he stopped the man from bullying and hurting one of his own students. When the man tried to retaliate by throwing punches, Mr. Miyagi only took one step to the right and one step to the left. The attacker wound up smashing both hands through car windows.

Well…actually, Mr. Miyagi did ONE other thing. He made the man think he was about to kill him…and then calmly pinched his nose…and walked away.]

Priceless. Priceless lesson. And here was another Danny…Daniel, actually…who was right there to take the lesson all in! As God is my judge!

And for your information, that's what the name, Daniel, means, by the way: "God is my judge."

Think about THAT.

[And I love what Miyagi says to answer Daniel's pointed question as they are walking away.

> **Daniel: You could have killed him, couldn't you?**
> **Miyagi: Aye.**
> **Daniel: Well why didn't you, then?**
> **Miyagi: Because, Daniel San, a person with no forgiveness in heart living even worse punishment than death.]**

NO ROOM IN THE HEART
Words and Music by – Roger Emerson

If you chose your friends with eyes closed,
You'd be in for a big surprise.
They'd be all sizes shapes and colors,
And they would make you realize

There's no room, no room for hatred!
No room, no room for biases of the heart!

If you took the time to know me,
You'd see we are much the same
What is it that you are afraid of?

Why can't we stop this senseless game?

There's no room, no room for hatred!
No room, no room for biases of the heart!

It'll be hard to change those things
Buried within your heart.
Make it a pledge to change the things
That we should never start!

No room, no room for hatred!
No room, no room for biases of the heart…
Of the heart…
Of the heart!

7. **Help African-American children connect to their own rich heritage.**

We will take a sample from a 2013 show called "Seeds of Greatness" as an illustration of this specific goal. Though our campers are culturally diverse, the majority are African American and occasionally this particular heritage is an emphasis in the shows.

Scene 1 – "Queen Mother on Birthing" – Sets up show

(Drummer(s) herald(s) the arrival of the Krobo Queen Mother who is about to work with a group of children. At Center Stage…from a stool…Queen Mother sits with children gathering around her.)

> Queen Mother: "Who can tell me how the birth date of a child is calculated?"

(Excited young hands from the tribal crowd are raised up.)

Child One: The birth date of a child is counted not from when it was born, and not from when its mother becomes pregnant, but from the day that the child was a thought in its mother's mind! And when a woman decides that she will have a child, she goes off and sits under a tree, by herself, and she listens until she can hear the song of the child that wants to come.
Queen Mother: "And THEN, what happens?"

(More excited young hands raised.)

Child Two: After she's heard the song of this child, she comes back to the man who will be the child's father, and teaches it to him. And then, when they start to physically conceive the child, some of that time they sing the song of the child, as a way to invite it.
Queen Mother: "Who can tell me more?"

(More hands raised after each of the continuing speeches.)

Child Three: When the mother is pregnant, the mother teaches her child's song to the midwives and the old women of the village, so that when the child is born, the old women and the people around her sing the child's song to welcome it. And then, as the child grows up, the other villagers are taught the child's song.

(Queen Mother points to another child without speaking.)

Child Four: If the child falls, or hurts its knee, someone picks it up and sings its song to it. Or maybe the child does something wonderful, or goes through tough times growing up, and as a way of honoring or supporting this young person, the people of the village sing his or her song.

(Queen Mother holds up her hand to stop Child Four from speaking further and points to another.)

Child Five: In our tribe there is also one other time when the villagers sing to the child. If at any time during his or her life, the person commits a crime or some terrible social act, the individual is called to the center of the village, the people in the community form a circle around them, and then they sing their song to them.

(Child Six is working extra hard to get the Queen Mother's attention, and she picks this child.)

Child Six: *(Speaking very crisply and properly)* Our tribe recognizes that the correction for antisocial behavior is not punishment; it is love and the remembrance of identity. When you recognize your own song, you have no desire or need to do anything that would hurt another.

(Everyone oohs and ahs in appreciation.)

Queen Mother: And I am sure you all know that it goes this way through a person's entire life. In marriage, the songs are sung, together. And finally, when this person is lying in bed, ready to die, all the villagers know his or her song, and they sing—for the last time—the song to that person. Yes?
All Children: Yes!
Queen Mother: And here is something else you should know: Even for those who have not grown up in an African tribe that sings your song to you at crucial life transitions, their lives are always reminding them when they are in tune with themselves and when they are not. They just have to pay attention!

When you feel good, what you are doing matches your song, and when you feel awful, it doesn't. In the end, we shall all recognize our song and sing it well. You may feel a little wobbly at first, but so have all the people who have worked to sing their song to greatness. What you have to do is just keep singing your own song of life, and you'll find your way home. Yes?

All Children: *(Extra excitedly)* YES!!!

(Narration below segues to song, "Nyame Upendo")

Narration 2

"Keep singing your own song of life and you'll find your way home."

There is no doubt about this. YOUR song of life is connected to your purpose…the reasons why you are on the planet…and this song…this identity is unique to you. Sing your song of life!

At the same time, though, there are songs we need to sing together…because we are all connected. In fact we are all related.

Now…there are people who don't believe in God. And those of us who do have LOTS of different ideas about God. But one thing most of us agree on is that we are all God's children; and as such we know this: "God loves you and me." Or put another way, "Nyame upendo we-we na me." *(Pronounced: ny-ah-may oo-pen-juh way-way nah may)*

And when we sing THAT song, it sounds like this.

Song 1

"Nyame upendo we-we na me."

Last, I think it is fair to assume that our consistent efforts allow us to make an impact on these other listed goals (at least) and more:

8. **Educate the masses about the historical contributions and accomplishments of African-Americans.**

IMITATION OF LIFE

9. Develop appreciative and creative listening and learning for all.

We have many evaluations with comments to back up the assumption that we have reached our goals. For example, we received 51 evaluations from a 2005 presentation to a high school group in which on a scale of 0 to 10, with 10 being the highest, we were rated above 9.25 for both education and entertainment. And high school students are often among the most critical of all the audiences we see. Attendees went on to say, in part:

- I liked the drumming and the music.
- Very fun, makes you feel good about yourself.
- Very empowering.
- I love the ending act. And the stories about Forest Idol and African Proverbs.
- I liked everything about the assembly—especially the music and their expressions. I hope you come back next year.
- I liked the music and the stories. It inspired me b/c I have to go read to some elementary school kids. And I also love to dance. Thanx.
- Stories were very informational! Thanx!
- That was awesome!
- I really enjoyed it and I found it very educational.
- This was a great event. It let us learn a lot today, and if nobody else didn't, I did. Thank you!

Let's come back to the script for "Seeds of Greatness" and let the opening narrator wrap up this chapter for us.

Seeds of Greatness Narration 1

Narrator: Seeds of greatness are EVERYWHERE! They are in books, in conversations, in classrooms, and on television. They are in songs, in flowers, in animals and bugs. They are in foods and muscles and sweat and the eyes and voices of friends. They are in tools and machines and wind and fire and musical instruments. They are in all the qualities that have made it possible for life of all kinds to exist on earth. They are in more places than you can possibly count.

The great challenge for all of us is to LOOK for seeds of greatness and help plant them and nurture them so they can grow in the places they are meant to be. And you will know where seeds of greatness are <u>meant</u> to be because they will grow and flourish in those places. Seeds of greatness that do not grow are either in the wrong place, they have the wrong gardener, or they simply remain undiscovered; but we can fix this.

This is what we do for each other—whether we are really trying to or not: We notice greatness, and then we look for the places from which that greatness grew, and we find the seeds. And when we find the seeds, many of us become farmers like the Maasai, The Krobo, The Kikuyu, and the Ga tribes in Africa. But we are not just farmers of vegetables, and fruits, and grains, and livestock; we are farmers of character and wisdom and strength and courage and perseverance. We are farmers of love and peace and creativity and cleverness. We are farmers of compassion and support and healing and worship. We are farmers of greatness!

As we may have heard, the oldest human remains have been found in Africa. The continent is often called the cradle of civilization. Understanding the traditions of a past that includes roots in Africa for all of us may be in someone's book or news report; and yet, when we look carefully, we can recognize the roots of this special something in all our families—from the first moment of our birth to the last moment of a life on earth.

And with that said, shall we see what seeds of greatness we can discover…here…and now?

Indeed. Shall we?

"Every child is an artist. The problem is how to remain an artist once we grow up."
—Pablo Picasso

"Acting is nothing more or less than playing. The idea is to humanize life."
—George Eliot

"Music is what feelings sound like."
—Author Unknown

"A tap dancer is really a frustrated drummer."
—Eleanor Powell

"Dancing is poetry with arms and legs."
—Charles Baudelaire

"Painting is poetry that is seen rather than felt, and poetry is painting that is felt rather than seen."
—Leonardo da Vinci

"I've probably romanticised it in my head, but I seem to remember that in the space of an hour's drama workshop, I was transformed. I went in really shy, and I came out full of confidence."
—Christian Cooke

"Logic will get you from A to B. Imagination will take you everywhere."
—Albert Einstein

"Imagination! Imagination! I put it first years ago, when I was asked what qualities I thought necessary for success upon the stage."
—Ellen Terry

"Because we are interested in promoting wellness, we will integrate medicine with performing arts, arts and crafts, agriculture, recreation, nature, and social service. Those are some skeletal parts."
—Patch Adams

"I believe so much in the power of performance I don't want to convince people. I want them to experience it and come away convinced on their own."
—Marina Abramovic

"The thing about performance, even if it's only an illusion, is that it is a celebration of the fact that we do contain within ourselves infinite possibilities."
—Daniel Day Lewis

"Act the way you'd like to be and soon you'll be the way you act."
—Leonard Cohen

"The world is a complicated place, and there's a lot of division between people. The performing arts tend to unify people in a way nothing else does."
—David Rubenstein

CHAPTER 10

Buckner TAPS (Teaching the Arts Performing School)

I ndeed, we *shall* see what seeds of greatness we can discover through our imitation of life explorations, and we'll begin to do so now, with a perfect segue between this chapter and the last.

So far in our investigation, we have traveled outside of school classrooms, and mostly in a world populated by older learners. This is about to change.

It changes for two reasons: (1) It is important to emphasize that the concepts, ideas and activities shared here are useful with actors of all ages, including those at the primary level. Every child is an artist, Picasso says. And (2) it is important to recognize this approach is equally effective whether applied outside of school settings or in the thick of them.

In this chapter, we will primarily explore some of the philosophies, strategies and programming applied over a twenty-five year period at the Mary Wadsworth Buckner Teaching the Arts Performing School in Wichita, Kansas also known as Buckner TAPS. Today, the performing arts aspect of this school is coupled with a focused exploration of the sciences and it's now called the Buckner Performing Arts and Science Magnet School.

Planting Seeds

For a performance piece to celebrate the Buckner School's 50th Anniversary, their Performing Arts Team brainstormed ideas that would best show what their program was about. They settled on the theme of planting seeds as a metaphor for their work in introducing the arts to children, recognizing their interests and abilities, and nurturing their skills and talents to fruition.

    A multi-media presentation was developed using film and music, along with live dance and mime. Through a venerable mother earth character on screen, the production depicted seeds being planted with a breath, then growing into children with various interests and proficiencies. With the brilliant help of a cinematographer, and Nick Johnson, head of the Wichita State University Department of Dance (who is also an accomplished performer and teacher of mime) the children were in and out of the principal scene, seamlessly appearing on stage and in the film.

    The kids loved it, the audience was mesmerized, and the central idea of Buckner's purpose in nurturing the artistic abilities of young children was successfully transmitted. It was also an exciting example of how one can start with a single theme idea and develop its message into an amazing performance piece through the vehicle of creative theater.

Everyday Kids, Teaming, and Creativity

For most of the content in this chapter, I am indebted to my wife, Denise Jackson-Simon, who built the only elementary level drama program and curriculum in the state of Kansas at Buckner, and taught the drama class for 23 years to all students who attended the K-5 school. As the drama instructor, she was joined by four other educators each year to form the Performing Arts Team, which included teachers of art, music, dance, and physical education.

    Now, before we go on, there are several points I must make.

One very important point of emphasis is that most of you reading this book will not be part of a program like the one which exists at Buckner—even if you are at the secondary level in a school district. Buckner is and has almost always been primarily a magnet program dedicated to its particular identity as a performing arts school. However, it is not and never has been a "Fame School."

Though there were highly talented kids who emerged occasionally in the flow of instruction at Buckner, students and their families applied based on their interests in the program, but they did *not* have to audition to attend. Probably, only those of you who are connected to post-secondary schools will identify with the interdisciplinary structure which has been characteristic of Buckner's program. However, even you will have access to the most talented and prepared students as opposed to working with students of all levels of interest and talent.

Secondly, this will offer a peek into Buckner's world, but it is not for the purpose of recommending that you build or advocate for this kind of program in your community...although if you are so inspired, we can guarantee that the benefits will be totally worth the effort it will take to establish such a program. Instead, we hope to highlight the kinds of teaming efforts and learning activities that can be creatively applied for meaningful projects in which the performing arts can be engaged to promote significant learning.

Third, even short of interdisciplinary or multi-classroom teaming or partnering, individual classroom teachers can apply the kinds of talents, strategies and activities highlighted in this chapter and previous ones to make learning come alive for students or other participants in ways that most standard instruction cannot. Fine arts, language arts, and social studies are subjects which fit best for some of these strategies, but science and math and other disciplines can also find ways to imitate life through the arts while engaging students in significant learning—as can non-academic settings.

Many readers, for example, will be familiar with the Schoolhouse Rock project which provided just this kind of creative, arts-related approach to learning. So has the iconic Sesame Street. Similar to this, my wife and I—independent of each other—also used theatrical and arts-related strategies in our regular classrooms early in our careers, and so have other teachers we have known. We've used everything from studying popular music in class, to performing plays or reader's theater, to creating raps as memory devices for rote learning, to inter-classroom competitions, to dressing up in costumes as characters from history (or having students do so), or acting out stories with movement or staging. The possibilities are endless for those willing to creatively explore them. It's about using our imaginations.

Now, let's look at another of the flagship projects at Buckner and see what we can learn or be inspired to create by being imaginative.

I See the Rhythm

Using the book, *I See the Rhythm,* by Michele Wood and Toyomi Igus, Buckner's Performing Arts team created a production which was performed by the school's 4th grade classes with the help of artists from the community.

The book is a visual and poetic introduction to the history of African American music. It includes art, poetic text, a description of musical styles, and a timeline of selected historical events. It also pays tribute to the musicians who gave the different forms of music its life.

One class of students created the flats for the background which depicted scenes from select years featured in the book. These were created as part of their art classes, and later installed on one of the school's walls as a feature. Another class used everyday items to create a percussion piece which was performed at the end of the show…a unit in their music class. The third class dramatized the action that went along with the poetry highlighting each musical style and its genesis as presented in the book, and different students recited the poetry. The historical timeline was also projected on screen throughout the performance.

This project was a fabulous example of arts integration. The students used math while creating the designs and compositions for the painted flats. Math was also integrated into the music lessons as they explored a variety of rhythms—a practical exercise in using fractions. Reading and social studies were a big part of the dramatic interpretation and overall exploration of music and historical events. And, of course, life skills including communication, decision making, and cooperation were all integral parts of the entire process.

The pride and self-esteem experienced by the students, though not measurable, were nonetheless, palpable. They came to school every day, begging to work on the project, and the culminating performance was a highlight for everyone that year.

Any number of folk tales, fables, fairy tales, nursery rhymes, children's stories, or other sources can be brought to life on the stage in the same manner. And within certain books or resources, you might actually find poetry which lends itself nicely to performance—perhaps presented in rap form to music or percussive rhythms, and performed as a solo piece or with a large choral group. Stories from books can be performed as reader's theater, or they can be narrated while actors dramatize the scenes in pantomime. Dialogue in books can serve as scripts with speaking parts already established. The ideas are endless and can be as simple as reciting poetry to engage students emotionally and perhaps kinesthetically…to fuller productions complete with music, dance, drama, or visual art.

Why Integrate the Arts?

Anyone who is interested can easily find a great deal of information on integrating the arts into academic learning. Many of the specific concepts, strategies and ideas that follow in this chapter, for example, can be found in a single resource: *The Arts as Meaning Makers: Integrating Literature and the Arts Throughout the Curriculum* by Claudia Cornett and Katharine Smithrim. Let's take a moment to highlight some of what you can discover in this resource and elsewhere. *(See the bibliography for other books and resources.)*

- The arts are fundamental components of all cultures and time periods.
- The arts teach us that not all of what we think, or feel, can be reduced to words.
- When students engage in the arts, they get to be smart in different ways.
- The arts actually develop the brain in ways other disciplines do not.
- The arts provide additional avenues of achievement for student success. ("Music is what feelings sound like"…"dancing is poetry with arms and legs.")
- The arts develop a value for perseverance, hard work, and excellence.
- The arts are a necessary part of life, as evidenced by its existence in every culture.
- There is a strong positive relationship between the arts and academic success.
- The arts offer alternative forms of assessment and evaluation.
- The arts can be a "feel good" alternative for students who turn to drugs and other destructive means to "get high."
- "Acting is nothing more or less than playing" and it "humanizes life," said George Eliot.

How Can Classroom Teachers Meaningfully Integrate the Arts?

We have touched on some of these strategies already, but let's be a bit more specific about how we can meaningfully integrate the arts into what we do.

Teaching *With* the Arts: Here we recognize that students get pleasure from the arts and enjoy having a chance to work creatively. (We have examined this idea in a variety of ways already in this book.) We

IMITATION OF LIFE

might also find that the arts are casually used by teachers in isolated lessons and may or may not be linked to curricular expectations.

For one example of the latter, consider this: On a couple of occasions as a junior high social studies teacher, I borrowed part of a comedy sketch by Richard Pryor, showed up in a pseudo-military costume, and introduced myself to my classes as "Idi Amin Dada, Ruler, President for Life, Uganda"—complete with an African accented British-tinged English. I doubt that any connection could have been made between this and the American History classes I taught, but it *was* connected to current events, and to the relationship I worked on building with my students. Both of these objectives mattered.

As another example, a former student of mine shared a memory not long ago of a unit I introduced in a class (probably one called "Issues and Society") in which each student was given an imaginary $500 budget to invest in the stock market however they chose. She still remembers the value of the thinking that went into choosing stock shares to buy, and monitoring their performance from week to week. This lesson could be considered a sample of role play at its finest. The role was as an investor, and yet, the only aspect that wasn't real were the dollars invested. Otherwise, it was clearly an example of what we are exploring here…an imitation of life!

When it comes to students getting pleasure from the arts and enjoying a chance to work creatively, it doesn't get better than a project called "Creating Original Opera," which students at Bucker had an opportunity to take part in. It was designed for schools by The New York Metropolitan Opera, and as part of the project, students were script writers, composers, performers, public relations managers, set designers and set builders, choreographers, dancers, and costume designers. They also served as co-directors who worked side by side with teachers, and even electricians who built foot lights and a small light board!

When I say possibilities are endless in creative theater, they really are. The only limit is your imagination, and last I checked, imagination still has *no* limits.

Teaching *About* and *In* the Arts: In Chapter 7, I mentioned an art history professor I had in college. He routinely held his classes spellbound week after week with absolutely fascinating lectures on the evolution of art forms through the experiences, talents and times of the artists who created them, and he was like a walking library of stories. It was clear that he loved the subject, but he was also very articulate, passionate and energetic, and had a great sense of humor.

Once when he had been lecturing for over an hour on the topic of the day, he stopped mid-sentence, smiled, and said, "I think you have reached your saturation point. Class dismissed." No doubt he had noticed that many of us appeared overwhelmed, our minds overflowing with details!

Students enjoy and develop both creativity and artistry when they are being expertly taught about or in the arts. When learning events focus on arts content and skills, there is a conscious effort to develop the aesthetic sensibilities of students through guided experiences. The art teacher becomes a coach to students who are involved in exploration, creation, response, performance, and evaluation, all while their experiences are tied to the required course of study.

I remember how a single lesson from a friend who taught the visual arts shifted me from a pencil artist to a painter. It happened when I popped into her classroom while kids were painting, and she invited me to come down and paint sometime. When I assured her that I was good at drawing but knew nothing about painting, she simply said, "If you can draw, you can paint." She slapped a blank canvas on an easel, grabbed a paint brush and a small jar of paint, and showed me the basics of how to "draw a bead" of paint with a steady hand. And then she handed me the brush and said, "Now you try it," and walked away.

Within minutes I was successfully doing what she showed me and decided on the spot to do an abstract project in her class on my off periods. It's hanging on the wall of my studio right now, and it was the first of several similarly conceived abstracts I ended up doing… and eventually gifting to others.

Teaching *Through* the Arts: When the arts are made prominent somehow through focused arts-related routines, an aesthetic classroom or workshop environment, as the content and the means of learning, or in units or activities specified by a curriculum or a set of objectives, learning magic can happen. Whether it involves creating a classroom in which students truly live and learn through the arts, or doing the same through providing opportunities to perform, the emphasis is still in teaching through the arts. The process of creating meaning using the arts, and the subject matter of each of the arts can still be valued and taught—even if in bits and pieces. The arts may also be used to teach other subjects.

General Principles for Integration

There are many possibilities for integrating the arts into educational objectives, and for numerous settings. Here are just a few to consider:

- Teach or explore arts concepts and skills whenever and wherever you can.
- Develop teacher or trainer habits that promote artistry, creativity, and independent meaning making.
- Use energizers and warm-ups to facilitate creativity, skill-building, and problem-solving processes.
- Mix the arts with literature of all kinds.
- Establish routines that both structure the experiences of performers you hope to influence and promote their independence in being able to influence others.
- Adapt important curricula or content with integration of the arts in mind.
- Plan arts-based field trips, workshops, or tutorials to extend learning as needed.
- Exhibit artistic creations to support the continuation of the approach and create performer/creator satisfaction.
- Use specialists as important resources for skill-building, ideas and support.

Skill and Talent Building for Arts Integration

The world of creative theater that Denise and I occupy has often been characterized by activities designed to contribute to imagination, self-confidence, poise, experience, and the nurturance of skills and talents. This is how excellence is built. It is a progression that moves novices to proficiency, and the proficient to outstanding. At the same time, however, beneficial experiences can be delivered to audiences regardless of the level of expertise of the performers. The key is to begin with the gifts and talents available in your pool of willing participants, and then polish them as often and as much as possible.

At the same time, discovering ways to connect artistry to the achievement of normally unrelated goals and objectives is as much or more a matter of giving yourself permission to do so, and setting an intention to follow through as it is in anything else.

What follows are some of the exercises that can be applied in service of this objective.

Practicing Greetings: In pairs or other configurations, simply practice greeting each other in an interaction that features any or all of the following: *Non-verbally, like old enemies, like long-lost friends, like young children, in a bored manner, with accents, like suspicious spies, like characters from literature, TV, or history, etc.*

Using Objects Differently: Using the same object, make it serve different purposes, or make it serve purposes that characters from a story, or a historical event would employ, or apply to any other topic that would lend itself to such an activity. *Stick, scarf, chair, plate, book, backpack or purse, pencil, cell phone, cardboard box, sheet of paper, etc.*

Dialogue Cards: Use words, phrases, or sentences from magazines or newspapers. Pairs can use cards to create dialogue; read cards expressively; line up and improvise verbal response that connects to the previous person by using what's on their card; or divide into two groups with questions asked, and whoever believes they can answer using their card, does so.

Tableau, A Frozen Picture: Using book titles, current or historical events, advertisement slogans, quotes from famous people, phrases from units of study, personal experiences, and so forth, small groups create tableaux with captions spoken or otherwise used to label the scene for others in the group or for an audience.

Simple Machines: Build a human "machine" with body movements and vocal or other sounds in groups of three or four (or more). *Could include a pulley, wheel and axle, hinge, lever-fulcrum, chisel, gear, wedge, inclined plane, screw, etc…and should accomplish some task, or simply demonstrate component connectivity.*

Just Walking: Walk different ways and through different environments: *Slow, fast, forward, backward, sideways, on tiptoes, on heels, through tall underbrush, through a dark alley, in the burning desert, in outer space, across a log over a ravine, through a snowstorm, through a swamp, across a street of chewed-up bubble gum, underwater, etc.*

Small Group Dance: Brainstorm different movements associated with one of the following topics and explore BEST dance elements that relate to the topic, shaping dance ideas with a beginning, middle and end. **(BEST** = The **BODY,** capable of motion, requires **ENERGY**, uses **SPACE**, and takes **TIME.)** Examples include the following. <u>Science</u>: *body systems, seasons and cycles, weather, environments, gravity, states of matter, energy, landforms, represent specific solar system aspects such as rotation and revolution.* <u>Social Studies</u>: *occupations, transportation, communities, housing, economies, etc.* (edutopia.org)

Choreography Sentences: Small groups choose six to eight "movement cards" and create a "dance" by putting the cards in sequence and moving accordingly.

Rainstorm: Create a sequence of sounds by rubbing hands together, snapping fingers, clapping hands, stomping feet *(slow to fast, soft to loud and reverse)*.

Music and Images: Participants listen to eight distinctive styles of recorded music. On a piece of paper divided into eight sections, they write or draw their immediate impressions, feelings, images, reactions, and how the music affects them.

Elements of Shape: Teams have one minute to find all the circles, dots, straight lines, angled lines, and curved lines they can find in a room.

Storytelling in a Box: Topics or themes are brainstormed or selected by a teacher or leader. Participants collect items from a suggested list or using their imaginations. Using elements of art, they create an assemblage in a small box around the theme, then write a short story or description for the presentation.

Writing Styles Rap: Create a poem around a concept being taught or studied, and set it to a rhythm.

There are so many more possibilities…just based on the history at Buckner alone, but the reflections and ideas shared here can serve as seeds of inspiration to get you started.

Feeling a little more ready for a takeoff?

"A few years ago, during an otherwise innocuous conversation, one of my oldest and dearest friends relayed the following story about her 17-year-old daughter: "Sophie [not her real name] and her boyfriend were at a party last weekend, and he got mad about something she said, and he literally picked her up by her shirt and threw her against the wall.

While the incident was shocking, it was Sophie's reaction—or lack thereof—that horrified me. Being body-checked by a boyfriend should have shaken her to the core, but Sophie didn't seem to consider it a big deal.

That's when I experienced That Parenting Moment, the one that flings us from the world in which we grew up into the unrecognizable reality where our kids are learning to live—and to love."

—From "Confront dating abuse through communication," Op-Ed by Lori Weinstein, Feb 17, 2010

"(Chris barges past Emma and walks into her room, visibly enraged and huffy, and she follows him.)

Chris: I bet you forgot I had your Facebook password huh? Just thought you were safe to flirt and cheat!?? Well you sure as heck aren't! Look! *(Chris tosses the printed message papers at her and begins to pace while she stares at them.)*

Chris: Am I not good enough for you? Do you even care about me? You know I would never do that to you!

(Chris goes and sits down with his head in his hands.)

Emma: I'm so sorry! I never meant anything by it! We were just talking! It doesn't matter! He doesn't matter! I'm sorry! Please forgive me! *Emma rushes to Chris and is touching his hands and arms. Chris pushes her down, and she just lays there on the ground astonished.*

Emma: *(Shocked)* **How could you?!**

Chris: How could I? You were flirting with another guy! What? You think you can just whore yourself around behind my back huh? Did you?!

Emma: That gives you no right to push me down like this! *(Standing)* **UH! Leave me alone! Get out! I cannot believe you would lay your hands on me!! That's just NOT right! Get out! Get out! GET OUT!!!** *(She is sobbing, and yelling at the same time, pointing Stage Right at the "door."*

Chris: No! *(Defiantly crosses arms)*

Emma: Yes, you need to leave now…Seriously I don't feel safe around you when you're mad. In fact, I don't think I can be around you period."

—From "Love, Not Lies," by Jennifer Grey, Macyn Gracy, Rachelle Feuillerat, Teens About Prevention, March 2011

CHAPTER 11

Improv Revival – Start Strong Wichita

It is hard enough for parents to begrudgingly admit that their children are growing into adults, but the details of what this means when it is genuine can add layers of complexity that are overwhelming. Not only do their children's hormones start to rage as adolescence rears its demanding head, but kids must negotiate motivations and challenges. Peer relationships are more problematic, temptations abound, and the march toward sophistication for tweens and teens often outstrips their evolution into maturity of thoughts, feelings and actions, and the skills that can help kids navigate them.

One of the *last* things parents want to find out is that their child is being victimized by relationship violence—whether it is physical, emotional, or both. But it happens, and it is best to be prepared rather than surprised.

Meanwhile, young people are often aware of the kinds of violence that can emerge within relationships, at least when it is happening outside of their own experience. When it is emerging in their own encounters, however, it is often obscured by the kind of emotional components that can only appear when connections take a more serious or intimate turn. Sadly, many young people are ill-prepared unless they have excellent models for healthy relationships with which they can identify. Otherwise, they are likely to find their models in the media or in their peer group...and both of these sources are highly suspect because of their shallowness and/or the fact that escalated conflict (however contrived) "sells better" than struggles minimized.

These realities were the inspiration for the launch of the Start Strong Initiative in 2008.

Start Strong: Building Healthy Teen Relationships was a national program of the **Robert Wood Johnson Foundation** (RWJF, www.rwjf.org), the **Blue Shield of California Foundation** (BSCF, www.blueshieldcafoundation.org) and the organization that became **Futures Without Violence**. For four years these groups collaborated to apply an $18 million investment in eleven (11) Start Strong sites nationwide. The project promoted healthy relationships among 11- to 14-year-olds and worked on developing strategies to prevent teen dating violence—which research had determined would often have its roots in relationships that started to emerge before kids arrived in high school.

The eleven Start Strong Sites which won grants were **Atlanta, Austin, Boston, Bridgeport, Bronx, Idaho, Indianapolis, Los Angeles, Oakland, Rhode Island,** and **Wichita.** The core components of the Start Strong program were to:

1. **Educate and engage youth in schools and out of school;**
2. **Educate and engage teen influencers such as parents/caregivers, older teens, teachers and other mentors;**
3. **Change policy and environmental factors; and to**
4. **Implement effective communications and social marketing strategies.**

It was in Wichita that I had an opportunity to be part of a small team of talented and creative facilitators who teamed up to meet the Start Strong objectives. We developed, distributed and applied curricula, organized band concerts and rallies, and supported already established Choose Respect Clubs while helping to launch others.

We took timely advantage of current events as teaching moments using episodes such as the Twilight movie trilogy (launched after the popularity of the books), and the very public relationship difficulties of pop stars Chris Brown and Rihanna. And we also developed a powerful improv performing troupe as an offshoot of a group of high school student leaders for Start Strong Wichita called **TAP (Teens About Prevention).** All of these served as launching points to talk about the differences between healthy and unhealthy relationships, and to promote the former.

Thanks to the independent research firm, RTI International, there was significant evaluation of the Start Strong program. The resulting assessment became one of the few, and the largest, studies to delve deeply into healthy relationship development and teen dating violence prevention efforts involving middle school students.

Though the funding stream for Start Strong evaporated after its four-year run, vestiges of its successes live on in the minds, hearts, and practices of those who participated, and also thanks to Futures Without Violence. You can learn more about Start Strong's sustainability at this URL: http://startstrong.futureswithoutviolence.org/about/. The site is a great resource for work with teens on dating violence prevention with a number of great lessons to share, insights about the most useful strategies and how to apply them, and some of the work that is ongoing in many of cities either because of Start Strong, or because grants provided a kick start for programs that were already in place. Such programs include RJOY in Oakland, Expect Respect in Austin, and Choose Respect Clubs in Wichita.

The Revival Begins

Though the Wichita program achieved measurable and acknowledged successes with the majority of our activities, it may well have been the improv troupe that achieved the greatest consistency and notoriety over the four-year project period. Once again, the use of creative theater proved invaluable in getting the attention of audiences everywhere, and it also provided opportunities for enlightening conversations with audience members of most ages.

The one drawback of our improv model, historically speaking, and against which I will caution you, is that we did not make a concerted effort to keep a record of the many skits and vignettes we performed. There are videos here and there, and a handful of scripts or outlines, but apart from these and the ones that stick out in the minds of those of us who produced them, many have been lost. Given a chance to try again, we would do better with this record-keeping aspect. Still, there are some that none of us will ever forget.

One of them was part of a project we were invited to do at Wichita State University by friend and professor, Jodi Hertzog, featuring our improvs as "interruptive stunts." This is what former troupe member Macyn Gracy rightly and synonymously calls a "flash mob type skit," because with this strategy the stage and performers are and can be anywhere.

The idea was to help raise awareness of relationship violence on campus where Dr. Hertzog and her students were organizing concurrent activities and events for which our team's contribution was a complement. Our actors performed several scenes at different public spots on campus, and they all got attention, but one in particular became our hit. Macyn remembers it this way, speaking from her perspective as one of the principal actors in the skit duo:

> **My "boyfriend" [a male actor] and I were in the commons area with the other students and we were just hanging out. Then he decided he wanted to leave and I didn't. I wanted to stay and eat some lunch and he got mad and started verbally abusing me about my weight, going where I'm told, and he started yanking my arm trying to pull me with him. He was loudly berating me, and I was exclaiming in distress. In one of the rounds we did this, one woman noticed the commotion and leapt to my defense. She actually hopped over the back of**

a couch that was between her and us to be able to physically intervene!

I was one of the lead facilitators with ultimate responsibility for the safety of our actors, as well as any spectators, and so I was present for this skit. We quickly "called it"—meaning that I stepped in to introduce and identify our group, explain what we were doing, and begin the processing for those who were unknowingly our audience members. I distinctly remember that the young woman who intervened was very small in stature, much smaller than Macyn or the male actor with whom she was working. Nonetheless, not only did she vault over the sofa, but she had her cell phone in her hand and clearly announced to the aggressive male, "You need to stop, or I'm going to call security!"

This was actually what we hoped would happen. With our Start Strong group, we were promoting the idea of people being "upstanders" rather than bystanders when witnessing abusive behavior. I can't imagine that anyone who saw this skit could have missed the point. And that *was* the point. This particular performance was the most dramatic example of one or more individuals standing up for the downtrodden, but we were generally successful in delivering the message to our audiences, and that was what we wanted.

Former TAP Troupe member Samantha Strahler remembered another presentation that was a group favorite…and it was one of our shorter skits in terms of duration. Samantha stated the following:

> **It was a skit of about fifteen seconds about four girls in a locker room. Each of them make comments about the others. It starts with one girl getting her bra strap popped as a joke, and she gets offended, but then comments about how another girl doesn't have straps because she doesn't even have boobs. Everyone laughs…and so on, with things like that.**

Once again, like the ten-second "Bitch Skit" described in Chapter 5, this scene takes far less than a minute to perform, but the audience can explore many factors and discuss various points, such as:

- Where does the scene take place, and how does the audience know?
- Can the audience relate to the setting…or translate it to another setting with which they are more familiar?
- Who is "in" and who is "out" among the girls, or is everyone fair game?
- Is any girl obviously more upset about the teasing, and if so, why?
- Where does this behavior come from? Is there a ring leader that everyone is trying to impress? If so, is she as confident as she wants the others to think she is?
- What does the audience imagine happens next with one or more of the girls…and what are the clues?
- Are any of the girls fully conscious of what they are really doing with the insults and barbs they trade?
- What might the audience discern about the history between these girls based on the dialogue, and what happens next?

Samantha also shared her opinion that "every skit was awesome! They were unique, and they presented different scenarios about the same issue that really helped people to understand the problem on a deeper level. It was fun and super relatable."

I have to agree. The issue was relationship violence and we chose to reflect realistic examples because they came directly from our actors' personal experiences, or situations they had witnessed.

In another scene that was a troupe favorite, no words were spoken. Instead, the message was carried by the lyrics to a rock song called "Face Down" by a band called The Red Jumpsuit Apparatus, and actions were made silently…or mimed, if you will. We played a recording of the song and created a live rendition of what the song related.

IMITATION OF LIFE

Look at this excerpt from the lyrics, and imagine how actors might mirror what you see in the words, including which characters would be speaking, and to whom, and how the story might end:

> Hey, girl, you know you drive me crazy.
> One look puts the rhythm in my hand.
> Still, I'll never understand why you hang around.
> I see what's going down.
>
> Cover up with make up in the mirror.
> Tell yourself it's never gonna happen again.
> You cry alone, and then he swears he loves you.
>
> Do you feel like a man
> When you push her around?
> Do you feel better now, as she falls to the ground?
> Well I'll tell you my friend, one day this world's
>   got to end.
> As your lies crumble down, a new life she has found.
> A pebble in the water makes a ripple effect.
> Every action in this world will bear a consequence.
>
> If you wait around forever, you will surely drown.
> I see what's going down.
> I see the way you go and say you're right again.
> Say you're right again.
> Heed my lecture.
>
> Face down in the dirt,
> She said, "This doesn't hurt."
> She said, "I finally had enough."
>
> > —Ronnie Winter

If you want to compare what you're visualizing in your mind to what the TAP kids created, you can probably still do so by seeing this video on YouTube from a live show produced by Start Strong Wichita:

https://www.youtube.com/watch?v=9xZ5fDcmAUY

One of our group's longer skits was one we called "Seven Times," which ironically lasted about seven minutes. It was inspired by a statistic we discovered which reported that a woman will leave and return to her abuser an average of seven times before she finally escapes…or (as it happens in far too many cases) is killed.

According to the TAP "hive mind," we think we performed the scene a couple of different ways, but essentially the events of abuse always started small—such as with verbal attacks, and then escalated to things like arm grabbing, or pushing, shoving or slapping, and then ended with the abused female being dragged off stage by her hair. Another included element was that many of the episodes occurred in front of the victim's friends and they tried to talk the sufferer out of the relationship. This gave the performers several opportunities to demonstrate some of the methods abusers use to manipulate the way that victims think and react.

Five Minutes, One Word

Finally, let's examine one of the few improvs we performed that was actually scripted because (1) it is abstract, and (2) we wanted it to be consistent every time it was performed. Here is a copy of the script, which is the only other script presented with just one single word of dialogue:

IMITATION OF LIFE

"Bitch" — A Silent Abstract Improv

> **BLOCKING:** The stage or staging area is to be considered split in half, Stage Left (SL) & Stage Right (SR). Except for entrances, all of the action described below takes place on both halves of the stage basically with "mirrored" or "cloned" blocking unless otherwise noted. The action is also mimed or carried out with movement, but no spoken dialogue except where otherwise noted. No props are necessary, but two may be used as indicated below. Otherwise the characters and settings should be created entirely with mime.
>
> The action from the start should be understood as beginning "In a Hallway at School with Teenagers," and ending some years later in "Two Separate Households," with appropriate settings in between.
>
> Three female and three male actors are required. Two male actors make their entrances from SR while two female actors enter SL. The third male actor stands upstage center (UC) in the SL half of the stage while the third female actor stands UC in the SR half…just behind the level where the other actors will interact…and with their backs turned and heads bowed. (NOTE: The third actors should have the skills (and preferably the appearance) to be believable as small children and as "adults.")

Two boys enter SR and two girls enter SL simultaneously, interacting with each other. Boy Pair and Girl Pair should separate in some creative and contextual way so that one of each pair stops midway of the half of the stage where they entered. (Ex. Horseplay, brief stop at locker, drink of water, etc.)

As the other of each pair continues across the stage, the character still moving interacts with the character that stopped briefly in this way: They <u>pass</u> each other, but <u>notice</u> each other with obvious interest, then turn 180 degrees and <u>meet</u> each other.

The two new Boy/Girl pairs start a mimed "conversation" with obvious "turn-taking" back and forth. They smile and laugh as they "talk," enjoying each other for about 15 to 20 seconds, move closer as they talk for the next five to 10 seconds, then touch each other in some innocent way at least twice in the next 10 to 15 seconds, ending with a brief, gentle, friendly hug.

They walk away from each other slowly in the directions they were originally moving, appearing to be deep in thought until they get to the edges of their half of the stage. They then walk slowly backward as if a recording is rewinding until they bump into each other midway. They slowly turn and face each other, smile, take both of each other's hands and slowly "dance" in a circle that way for about 15 to 20 seconds, "talking" again (adjusting slightly to be more centered if necessary), and ending with the Girl standing SR of the Boy after which they engage in a much longer hug.

Following the second hug, they turn toward the audience smiling and holding hands (Girl's left in Boy's right) and all six actors hum the first two measures of the classic Wedding March.

Following the "wedding," the two pairs face each other again and rip into a very energetic hug for five to 10 seconds that suggests the beginning, middle, and quiet end of passion. They separate and turn to face the audience again…smiling…with the Male slightly behind the Female as she mimes rocking a baby in her arms while he looks on.

After just a few seconds of this image, the smiling pair separates as if they are on opposite sides of a baby bed and with an audible sigh (Ex. Oh, Ah, Mmmm, etc.); the mother places the "baby" in the "bed" as both parents bend to caress it.

Simultaneously, the third actor on each side gracefully gets into a position between them to appear as a "toddler" sitting on the floor just beneath where they were caressing the baby in bed, and they now briefly caress the child.

(NOTE: Here, the Boy and Girl can have a "vehicle toy" and a "baby doll" respectively which they will be holding as they wait to enter. This, also, subtly demonstrates how children are socialized differently.)

Each set of parents then stands behind their child looking on adoringly for a few seconds before they begin a "conversation" in the same way that their first one was structured, taking turns back and forth for a total of about 20 seconds or so. The difference, though, is that the parents of the Boy Child go from pleasant smiles and normal conversation to very angry faces and heated conversation in the last

IMITATION OF LIFE

third of their exchange—ending with the Male slapping the Female and snarling the word "Bitch"…while the other parents are watching their Girl Child more than they are "talking" and by the time the slap happens with the other pair they have ended in a pleasant embrace still basically watching their daughter at play.

Both sets of parents freeze, and the audience now focuses on the children at play with their toys for 10 to 15 seconds, at the end of which you see that the Boy Child experiences some technical difficulty with his toy. He immediately bangs it angrily away and says "Bitch" in exactly the same way his father had.

After the angry word is heard the second time, the two sets of parents turn their backs to the audience and bow their heads while the two children rise from their sitting positions in a slow, graceful spiral until they are standing upright…and in the process have taken on body language and mannerisms which suggest they have grown up, and into teenagers.

At this point the two teens repeat the exact same "Dance of Acquaintance and Love" that the parents did, only much faster—up through the "Wedding." After the Wedding, we see the same "passion" hug—but not the baby. Instead, the couple does their own version of engaging in an after-passion "conversation" that goes from pleasant smiles and normal tones to very angry faces and heated exchanges in the last third of their conversation—ending with the male slapping the female and snarling the word "Bitch."

The two actors freeze, then slowly turn toward the audience and bow their heads.

The END

Processing follows…

…and we are on to the next chapter.

"If not YOU, WHO? If not HERE, WHERE? If not NOW, WHEN?"
—Unknown

"The only thing necessary for the triumph of
evil is for good men to do nothing."
—Edmund Burke

"Do all the good you can,
By all the means you can,
In all the ways you can,
In all the places you can,
At all the times you can,
To all the people you can,
As long as ever you can."
—Attributed to John Wesley, Founder of Methodism

"Never doubt that a small group of thoughtful, committed, citizens
can change the world. Indeed, it is the only thing that ever has."
—Margaret Mead

"You never change things by fighting the existing reality. To change
something, build a new model that makes the existing model obsolete."
—R. Buckminster Fuller

"The country is so wounded, bleeding, and hurt right now. The
country needs to be healed—it's not going to be healed from the top,
politically. How are we going to heal? Art is the healing force."
—Robert Redford, National Arts Policy Roundtable 2012

"Unless someone like you cares a whole awful lot,
Nothing is going to get better. It's not."
—Dr. Suess, *The Lorax*

CHAPTER 12

Creative Theatrics: Why You, Why Here, Why Now?

I once wrote a radio essay to assert that in the process of discovering the highest possible good in human relationships, the lowest common denominator leaves much to be desired. And yet that is what marketers, entertainers, and politicians often promote. I tried to make a case, instead, that we should contribute heroic effort to discover a highest common denominator—meaning (as Webster might put it) "the greatest possible number of shared human characteristics." As people who share a planet, what would be the result of continuing to search for a highest common denominator? I believe the benefits might literally be immeasurable.

Explore something with me for a moment. Let me ask you a pointed question: Could the following list of fifty items all be things that we have in common?

1. We are all humans alive on the earth.
2. We all have the same basic needs of food and water, clothing and shelter.
3. We all need love.
4. We all sincerely want to be the best we can be.

5. We all live our lives without ever realizing our full potential.
6. We all tend to want the best for those we love—especially children.
7. We all *want* to be loved.
8. We all have a powerful instinct for survival.
9. We all appreciate beauty as we see it.
10. We all want our own beauty to be appreciated as human beings.
11. We all want to be happy.
12. We all want to be successful.
13. We all want to be productive.
14. We all want to be free, and we sincerely want others to be free.
15. We all respond positively when we are truly loved.
16. We all are curious.
17. We all have an enormous capacity to learn.
18. We all want to be touched deeply by someone or something.
19. We all really *want* to get what we need without taking from others.
20. We all would never choose to be violent if we fully understood how to avoid it.
21. We all are ultimately a mystery to ourselves.
22. We all find others equally if not more mysterious.
23. We all recognize some power that is greater than us.
24. We all are attached to someone or something.
25. We all have expectations of our experience—sometimes unfair ones.
26. We all believe in justice but sometimes feel that we don't get it.
27. We all are often blinded by our own point of view.
28. We all believe in reality but don't truly know what it is.
29. We all are amazed by something.
30. We all have dreams.
31. We all are creative.
32. We all are all selfish to a degree.

33. We all value family at some level.
34. We all have an impulse towards altruism—caring for others.
35. We all enjoy music and art.
36. We all like to eat, drink and be merry.
37. We all have more questions than we do answers.
38. We all would like a chance to spend a million dollars on things that matter to us.
39. We all have a biological urge to make babies.
40. We all like discovering new things.
41. We all get excited about SOMETHING.
42. We all have things we will never forget…and some we wish we could.
43. We all are familiar with something that we would call perfect weather.
44. We all have something of which we are afraid.
45. We all tend to seek pleasure and try to avoid pain, which we all experience.
46. We all can do evil acts under certain circumstances, environments or motives.
47. We all are ultimately clueless about our ultimate origins.
48. We all believe some things strongly for which we have no proof.
49. We all have difficulty admitting the possibility of being wrong in what we hold true.
50. We all disagree with some of the things on this list.

Now, let's shift gears for a moment, and see if you can agree that we have a lot of these things in common. And let's also assume that there are many more things outside of this list on which we could probably agree. If either or both of these assertions are true, then why is it that we often behave as if *none* of them are true? And how important might it be for those of us who recognize this as a likely truth to promote it in some way?

We are so much more alike than we are different. We will also sink or swim as a species together…and our planet's survival as a hospitable place depends on our mutual collaboration. And yet, there are too many of us who still believe that our best chance of survival comes from the attitude of everyone for himself or herself, and that benefit for some of us must come at the expense of others. To make matters worse, there is a sense of entitlement for many of us that discounts the value of the rest of us.

And still…there is a hypothetically super impressive list of commonalities that we are considering that begs this question: How can we possibly judge who is deserving and who is not when science has proven again and again that we are essentially identical in terms of human value, and that we have many of the same capabilities and many of the same needs and desires?

In my humble opinion, this is a good place to begin to make the case that as many of us as possible should find and employ powerful ways to promote and facilitate learning that amplifies the quality of life for all. Creative and improvisational theatrics definitely fits the bill—for both efficiency and effectiveness.

To Engage and Interact

All the arts are powerful, and the forms we have been exploring here can be highly engaging and interactive as well, which makes them even more potent. With such uniquely innovative enactments, you can facilitate the kinds of insights and conversations that create leverage for achieving increased understanding and empathy among those who witness what you produce. There is so much need for this, and only limited amounts of time, energy, and resources that can be applied to meeting the need when someone volunteers. Getting the most possible leverage is key.

In helping professions, it doesn't seem to matter whether people are educators, counselors, social workers, therapists, law enforcement officials, attorneys, healers, ministers, or something else; what matters is how deeply they are committed to genuinely helping people. The same understanding applies to the strategies we are promoting here. If you are deeply committed to helping others, I encourage you to seriously consider doing so with these kinds of scene-making and discussion leading approaches—no matter what kind of helper you are. Do WHAT you can, for WHOM you can, WHILE you can, and know when you CANNOT.

To do what you can means just that...and no more. But I will remind you that if you are doing your best, no one can expect more from you than that. I believe you will be very favorably surprised at what you can accomplish by just making efforts to the best of your abilities and by inspiring the greatest efforts of those whom you would hope to lead.

Each of us has unique combinations of talents, abilities, skills, and unique opportunities to apply them. As we use them, we sharpen our capabilities and those of others; this results in all of us becoming more capable. That's good news. So, go ahead and use what you have and do what you can. That's the ticket! No more. No less.

Doing for <u>whom</u> you can is also governed by opportunities, limits, and challenges. There will always be those that we cannot reach or touch, or cannot help if we do touch them. Still, to do what you can for whom you can also means to take advantage of the legitimate opportunities you have to make a difference for anyone you can draw into an audience of any size—including an audience of one.

Last, you must do what you can <u>while</u> you can and know when you cannot. When I use myself as an example, there have been fluctuations in how the circumstances of clock and calendar have afforded me opportunities to put these kinds of strategies to work. As I have told you stories here, I recognize in retrospect that incidences of my own forays into available or targeted arenas for creative theater can be loosely identified according to decades...but not continuously. Specifically, beginning in the seventies, there has been some version of this approach I have personally activated for almost every single decade—not counting the current one. As of this writing, however, there is still time to make it five for five before 2020...and a very likely place it could occur. Maybe this is another time when I can.

YOU. HERE. NOW.

If you have gotten this far, know that this chapter is about YOU, HERE, NOW. This is about you recognizing that you can be one of the <u>good</u> people who can do <u>something</u> and exert an <u>amazing leveraged influence</u> in opposition to the evils of the world. You can do this as a leader, as part of whatever small committed group of people you can encourage to join you.

This is about helping to build a new model for what theater can be in the communities in which you serve. It won't make other forms obsolete…and it doesn't need to…but it can certainly become a deeply appreciated and beneficial aspect of the theatrical canon. And you can be a pioneer in making that happen.

If you accomplish nothing more than giving people unexpected and useful glimpses into worlds they would otherwise never see or understand, you will have worked a wonder. People make assumptions all the time about other people who live in situations or worlds they know nothing about. Under normal circumstances, they most certainly cannot appreciate these other conditions in any empathic way without being able to peek into the lives that feature them. Creative theater gives uninformed viewers opportunities to become the invited voyeur, and witness interactions of characters they might, otherwise, never see or know…and to learn from them.

What can a person who has enjoyed empowering relationships for a lifetime know, for example, about oppressive personal and family connections? What can an independently wealthy individual possibly understand about those who live paycheck to paycheck and who may regularly have too much month left over after a month's salary is depleted? How can a Muslim or Hindu be familiar with the life and times of a Christian or Ba'hai? Can a man who has spent years immersed in locker rooms with other men truly comprehend the worldview of a woman who has never been in *any* locker room or previously associated with someone who has?

Does an only child have a clue about daily life for a kid in a family of eight…or vice versa? Can a woman who has worked as a groundskeeper for twenty years relate to the world of one who has spent a career in an office? Would a shy pre-teen benefit from examining aspects of a confident person's life who was once a similarly shy pre-teen? If we see a small group of male characters on stage listening to a joke that begins, "A black man, a white man and a Mexican walk into a bar..." might people in the audience learn something about stereotypes or cultural sensitivity by listening to how the group responds after the punch line is delivered?

I believe the case is substantially made in these pages for believing that all of these questions can be answered in positive ways through creative theater. And why would it be important to help viewers answer these kinds of questions? I can think of two excellent answers beyond the obvious one of gaining useful information.

One answer has to do with the fact that some of the same folks who are isolated from the real experiences of people unlike them are often in positions of power and influence that can make these unknown worlds either better or worse. The world is full of examples of those who are truly powerful influencing decisions that can discount whole groups of individuals, destroy supportive institutions, demonize people or lifestyles simply because they are different, maintain oppression of the disadvantaged, or literally cause death and destruction. On the other hand, gaining proper insight about the lives of others can help create a world characterized by the absolute antithesis of every outcome sketched in the previous sentence.

A second reason to help people understand unexplored worlds of the human condition through theater is that people also know much less than they think they do about their *own* worlds. Sometimes it is a deeper examination of the circumstances most familiar to us that can be of great benefit.

Do we know why and how we come to believe what we believe? Are we confused about the difference between facts or "truth" as compared to a well-articulated opinion that may not be fact-based? Is intuition as legitimate as logic? Is discernment as powerful as deliberation? Do apathy or complacency have roots we can uncover? Which is more powerful—our thoughts or our emotions? Can we act our way into a different way of being? Can we see ourselves better if we are reflected in the behaviors of a character on stage?

The imitation of real life in theater can help generate insights, answers, new thoughts, or perhaps better questions…and all of these and more can help us become better human beings.

As Robert Redford has asserted, our country (and the world in general, I would add) is wounded, bleeding, and hurting. Additionally, the political structure is failing us in large part because it is serving the interests of those who are already in power as opposed to those the government is supposed to serve—its citizens. Art will not take the place of politics…because wherever there are people, we will find politics; but it can certainly enhance the strategies of those who would employ politics to leverage more inclusion for all. It can also hold accountable those who vie for leadership, as well as those who are charged with holding leaders accountable to the vast majority of us. And this clear majority includes everyone who simply wants personal freedom within a mutually constructed society, and the support of that same community in ways that allow us to live fulfilled lives.

So, take it from Dr. Seuss, and realize that nothing is going to get better unless someone like you cares "a whole awful lot." And if we want to truly make things better based on our caring, there are no more potentially powerful tools we can use than the potent theatrical ones we are discussing here.

"In times of change, learners inherit the earth, while the learned find themselves beautifully equipped to deal with a world that no longer exists."
—Eric Hoffer

"Human beings arrive in this world without capabilities and have to acquire them in an apprenticeship. The last half of [the 20th] century has seen massive changes in our culture which have undercut the family's ability to provide opportunities for young people to engage in an apprenticeship of habilitation to prepare them for life."
—H. Stephen Glenn

"It's what you learn after you know it all that counts."
—John Wooden

"Keep learning; don't be arrogant by assuming that you know it all, that you have a monopoly on the truth; always assume that you can learn something from someone else."
—Jack Welch

"Fyodor Dostoevsky predicted that at first art would imitate life, then life would imitate art, and finally, that life would draw the very reason for its existence from art."
—Ravi Zacharias, *Can Man Live Without God* (Dallas: Word Publishing, 1994) p. 73

"Life imitates Art far more than Art imitates Life"
—Oscar Wilde, 1889 (From his essay "The Decay of Lying")

"Among students assigned by lottery to see live theater, we find enhanced knowledge of the plot and vocabulary in those plays, greater tolerance, and improved ability to read the emotions of others."
—Jay P. Greene

CHAPTER 13

Life Imitates Art

Life often imitates art. And though some may surmise that this is a complete <u>reversal</u> of an old truism, I believe it to be just as true as its opposite—if not more so. I am not the only one who believes this. I think life has always imitated art. With art, creators can and do represent ideals, and these ideals can inspire any of us…or all of us…to reach for more. Art can also encourage us to narrow our definitions of what *is* ideal. That's a danger, and also another story.

Because of the influences of modernity—particularly through a plethora of media outlets and numerous expressions in entertainment and marketing—there's much to examine and criticize as it relates to life imitating artists' conceptions of what is presented (and may be perceived) as reality. Consider the long-promoted airbrushed and photo-shopped unnatural images of women in fashion media as a prime and troubling example. Sometimes life's imitations are not only short on accuracy, but also detrimental.

I have made a case for this observation before. I was a classroom teacher, for example, when Pink Floyd released their album entitled "Another Brick in The Wall." I even played the song on occasion using a stereo receiver and turntable I kept tucked in a closet in my classroom. I can't tell you how many times I witnessed kids exuberantly singing the first line of the song: "We don't need no education." I knew for a fact that some of them never really listened with understanding to the rest of the song. *Voila!* A teaching moment!

I took advantage of opportunities to explain that the band was really speaking out against "thought control" and "dark sarcasm in the classroom" and the promotion of young people performing to questionable societal norms they had nothing to do with creating. I had no problem awakening them to these insights or modeling positive alternatives.

Then there was the "I love you, man!" phenomenon kicked off by a classic Bud Light commercial on TV. After the commercial took hold, I often heard some guy jokingly (or seriously) say that very same phrase…with the same inflection…and I could swear this rarely happened before the commercial.

In another time period, I watched the rhythmic movement called "head-banging" taking off in earnest after it was popularized by the cartoon characters, Beavis and Butthead. And then, fast forward to a later period in societal history, and you get the baggy, underwear-revealing clothing style called *saggin'* that was not really a fashion statement until "gangsta rap" artists began to dress that way under influence from certain elements of prison culture. Add to this list the dance crazes from the past such as the "Smurf" and the "Roger Rabbit," inspired by cartoon characters, and the same on-screen genre contributing songs regularly performed at weddings, as well as well-known voice characterizations that have shown up in everyday conversations.

Remember…like…the Valley Girls? *Ohmigod!* This probably would have stayed in the California valley that spawned them if not for mass media. After all, the term originally was indicative of upper-middle class girls from Los Angeles commuter bedroom neighborhoods during the 1980s. So why are their much-reflected expressions *still* everywhere over 30 years later?

Let's also recognize characterizations and expressions that have entered our everyday vernacular from Tyler Perry's Madea, Jim Carrey's Ace Ventura character, Clint Eastwood's Dirty Harry, and even from classic actors like James Cagney and Edward G. Robinson…though the latter may have been recycled through modern-day animation features for younger impressionable viewers.

We were once taught by a commercial to ask, "Is it live or is it Memorex?"

Nowadays, we could ask, "Is it life, or is it art?"

Art is Essential

Arthur M. Schlesinger, Jr. quoted former President John Kennedy as saying that fellow Presidents Lincoln and Roosevelt "understood that the life of the arts, far from being an interruption, or a distraction, in the life of the nation, is very close to the center of a nation's purpose—and is a test of the quality of a nation's civilization." If this kind of insight from our revered nation's leaders is not at least a nod to life imitating art, I can't imagine what is. And yet, the most important consideration is not whether this is true, but what art we will encourage people to emulate, and in what form. There is an apparent difference between what is experienced as a "live performance," and what is gleaned from books or films.

Researcher Jay P. Greene carried out a study with colleagues in which it was determined that students assigned by lottery to see live theater came away with a greater knowledge of the plots of the plays they witnessed, as well as the vocabulary used in the productions, and felt more empathy for and identification with the characters by comparison to what students learned through reading those works or by seeing film versions of them.

ROB SIMON

Stunts and Interruptions

This brings me to "stunt journalism," in which reporters take risks to get a story they otherwise would not get, or "immersion journalism" in which journalists actually embed themselves in a milieu to facilitate taking a report from shallow and basic to rich and nuanced.

As an example of the latter, consider H.G. Bissinger's exploration of Texas high school football in *Friday Night Lights*, which eventually became a TV series. Bissinger actually moved his family to Odessa, Texas and spent the entire 1988 football season observing high school football players, their families, coaches, and the townspeople in general to better understand the rural town's relationship to the football culture that grew up around the Permian Panthers team.

More along the lines of a "stunt" would be John Howard Griffin's efforts in creating *Black Like Me*, his personal true story of a white man living as a black man in the segregated South thanks to a process he used for darkening his skin. Griffin took large oral doses of the anti-vitiligo medication, *methoxsalen*, and spent up to fifteen hours under an ultraviolet lamp every day to become a brown-skinned man. Grace Halsell did basically the same thing to pen her insightful book, *Soul Sister*.

The lines quickly blur between what is life and what is art when you have people living a real experience that is also a role they are playing, and then having their very real experiences become projects for television or the silver screen. Is this life imitating art, or art imitating life, or both? Either way, it is powerful.

Interruptive stunts are yet another twist on this blurred horizon between life and art. It is a form of immersion theater in which everyday people become part of a theatrical experience that finds them essentially playing themselves, but they don't realize, at first, that they are also part of a staged event.

One very entertaining classic example of this is preserved in television archives from a hit show that began in the late forties and ran in some form for decades. It was called Candid Camera, and was originally created by Allen Funt to play harmless practical jokes on unsuspecting folks, and then capture the often hilarious results for appreciative TV audiences. On the one hand, the formula was highly amusing; on the other, viewers were not likely to be particularly edified by the experience of watching episodes.

An example more along the lines of what we are examining here would be a short feature that aired during the 2018 Rose Bowl football event. An enterprising group filmed a contrived scenario in which a broken-down automobile was clearly marked with the identity of a certain school and its football mascot to see if any rival fans would stop on their way to a scheduled contest to help…and they did. The experiment was also successful when they reversed the circumstances of the staged breakdown to represent the rival team. The group's point was to emphasize that the commonalities among people outweigh petty differences.

Again, is this life imitating art, or art imitating life? Either way, it is powerful.

> "During our peer to peer marketing efforts, we took to the streets and performed "interruptive stunts" in locations where there were a high number of teens out and about. These locations included shopping malls, skate parks, parades, and music concerts. We had two team members act out each script, which all depict an argument between two teens in a relationship. At the end of each script, the two team members performing, in conjunction with their incognito counterparts, stage a reveal in which they display That's Not Cool t-shirts and shout "That's Not Cool!" After this reveal, the actors engage the audience and explain the campaign."
>
> —From Scripts created by the Family Violence Prevention Fund in partnership with GTM, Inc.

Maximum Interruption!

ABC launched a television feature called "What Would You Do?"

With hidden cameras, host John Quiñones and his crew film ordinary people encountering situations in which they will either take intervening action, or decide that it's none of their business to do so. Often a decision (not unlike in real life) must first be made in a matter of seconds, and could be altered in the minds of some observers based on variables such as race, gender, religion or political identity of the people involved, or other aspects of their appearance or behavior. And when the circumstances change, sometimes the way others react changes, too.

What would you do if you witnessed a waitress being harassed by her manager, or a group of teens shoplifting small items in a store, a mother verbally berating a small child, or a seemingly drunk or high valet parking cars? These are easy questions, but the answers are not as simple.

For more examples that beg the same question, consider this excerpt from a list of scenarios from the show reported in a Wikipedia featured article:

1. **A flamboyant hair stylist destroys women's hair. Other clients see the interaction and try to rectify the situation.**
2. **On a sidewalk, three teenagers beat and taunt a homeless man in front of passersby.**
3. **Various children (different race in each vandalism) vandalize a car.**
4. **A grocery bagger with noticeable Down syndrome is insulted and yelled at by a shopper, who calls him a "retard."**
5. **Multiple men and women of varying races steal items from an open house showing.**
6. **A young pregnant woman offers her baby to two different couples.**
7. **A sketch artist creates bad drawings after the customers have already paid.**

8. Two army soldiers back from a war zone are not allowed to order alcohol because they are underage.
9. A little girl's nanny abuses the child by screaming at her, and calling her stupid in public.
10. A little girl's nanny gives her medicine to calm her down and put her to sleep in a café because she is acting up.
11. A young girl abuses her nanny by treating her like a maid.
12. A man tries to sell fake tickets to an unsuspecting customer. *(https://en.wikipedia.org/wiki/What_Would_You_Do%3F_(ABC_News_series)*

When scenes are aired as part of the show, Quiñones appears at the end of each of them to interview bystanders who witness the misbehavior and quiz them about their reactions…or lack thereof. There might even be relevant experts included afterward to watch video of the segments with the host to share perspectives about the "whys" behind the behaviors.

Here, you have the same elements we have been discussing in our exploration of creative theatrics…with one added element that we have not emphasized, and that is blurring the lines between performance and reality.

In this feature, there are scenes and discussion of them by members of the audience. These elements are indistinguishable from the portrait we have been painting, but we have only just now begun to explore immersive components. This is not because they lack potentially high relevance. They most certainly do, but maybe it is appropriate that we waited until the last chapter to introduce them. To include immersive elements is to add a level of complexity that is riskier and more difficult to manage. However, you absolutely should keep it visible on your theatrical horizon; you just shouldn't plan to begin there.

Theater...or Journalism...or Both?

In a 2008 issue of Columbia Journalism Review, author Daniel Weiss speaks of this approach as "the journalism that tweaks reality, then reports what happens." This is not our goal. Instead we could say we are exploring theater that <u>reflects</u> reality, and then invites participants to <u>discuss</u> what happens. In both instances, we stand to learn something from presenting scenarios. This is why everything on the continuum that includes both theater and journalism is fair game—as long as we are cautious to do no harm.

Weiss also tells the story of a fascinating example of this genre.

> "On a Friday morning…, a group of Washington, D.C. commuters played an unwitting role in an experiment. As they emerged from the L'Enfant Plaza metro station, they passed a man playing a violin. Dressed in a long-sleeved T-shirt, baseball cap, and jeans, an open case for donations at his feet, he looked like an ordinary busker. In reality, he was Joshua Bell, an internationally renowned musician. The idea was to gauge whether Bell's virtuosic playing would entice the rushing commuters to stop and listen.
>
> The experiment's mastermind was *Washington Post* staff writer Gene Weingarten, who had dreamed it up after seeing a talented keyboardist be completely ignored as he played outside another metro station. 'I bet Yo-Yo Ma himself, if he were in disguise, couldn't get through to these deadheads,' Weingarten says he thought at the time. Ma wasn't available to test the hypothesis, but Bell was.
>
> For three-quarters of an hour, Bell played six pieces, including some of the most difficult and celebrated in the classical canon. Of 1,097 passersby, twenty-seven made donations totaling just

over $30. Seven stopped for more than a minute. The remaining 1,070 breezed by, barely aware of the supremely talented violinist in their midst.

When Weingarten's account of the experiment ran in the *Post*'s magazine three months later, readers followed the narrative with rapt attention that contrasted starkly with the indifference of the commuters. The article was discussed on blogs and other forums devoted to classical music, pop culture, politics, and social science. Weingarten said he received more feedback from readers than he had for any other article he had written in his thirty-five-year career. Many were taken with the chutzpah of disguising Joshua Bell as a mendicant just to see what would happen. Others were shocked that people could ignore a world-class musician. Still others argued that the results were insignificant: rerun the experiment outdoors on a sunny day, they said, and Bell would draw a massive crowd.

…Working on a hunch that begs to be tested or simply struck with an idea for a good story, journalistic 'experimenters,' for lack of a better term, step out of their customary role as observers and play with reality to see what will happen. At their worst, these experiments are little more than variations on reality-TV operations that traffic in voyeurism and shame. At their best, they manage to deliver discussion-worthy insights into contemporary society and human nature. The very best, perhaps, serve up a bit of both." *http://archives.cjr.org/essay/what_would_you_do.php*

Weiss has much more to say about this "brand of social psychology" masquerading as "forms of investigative, immersion, and stunt journalism that have been practiced for more than a century." He even touches on the story of Nellie Bly going undercover to expose malpractice in psychiatric hospitals in 1887 and how it fundamentally foretold a similar 1972 project launched by David Rosenhan. Our "cultural fascination with how people behave in contrived situations," he suggests, is why something like "What Would You Do?" works. It works because (as Chris Whipple, the producer who conceived the series, refers to it) it is a "*Candid Camera* of ethics."

This makes me think of television shows such as the Law & Order franchise, in which the tales told often mimic true stories underneath the headlines of news outlets. And then I think about the utter flexibility of the Imitation of Life approach and how easily it can be focused on any issue a group wants to explore with an audience. It doesn't matter whether it is an advertised or expected presentation or one that comes as an absolute surprise to the audience—but with the latter, there are some advantages. Not the least of which is the powerful immersive factor.

If you go to YouTube and type in "That's Not Cool," you can find examples of interruptive stunts that have been a successful part of this noteworthy program to raise awareness of teen dating violence.

One of the script outlines for these stunts appears below. This one and others like it were created by the Family Violence Prevention Fund in partnership with GTM, Inc. You can find more samples of scripts at: https://thatsnotcool.com/wp-content/uploads/2015/10/ThatsNotCool-InterruptiveStuntScripts-1.pdf

PHONE ABUSE – CONTROLLING

MALE - HERO *(Almost yelling)*
What is wrong with you?

GIRL - NEMESIS *(Yelling)*
What's wrong with you, all I've been trying to do is get a hold of you and you haven't been picking up your phone. I told you when I call—you answer my call (demanding).

IMITATION OF LIFE

>HERO *(Almost yelling)*
We are not together anymore and even if we were, if you call and I don't pick up, it's probably because I'm doing something and just busy. Just give me a little space.

>GIRL - NEMESIS *(Yelling)*
I never agreed to our breakup and that's not the point! You still need to take my call. I don't care what's going on. It's just rude to not pick up the phone when you see my phone number in the caller ID.

>MALE - HERO *(Yelling)*
>*(Addressing individuals in the crowd)*
She keeps texting me and calling me and I have no interest in talking to her. We are no longer together. Have you ever dealt with something like this? This is unbelievable!!!

>GIRL - NEMESIS *(Yelling)*
>*(Cuts their conversation off in a rude manner)*
Don't ask them anything; this is about you and me. I know you told me that it's over, but I don't care what you want. I can make this relationship work by myself.

>MALE - HERO *(Yelling)*
That's controlling…
(Yelled by entire team)…and "THAT'S NOT COOL!"

With this kind of skit, if it is believably performed, it is not until the very last line that the audience realizes they have been duped. Once they get past the shock, however, it's the discussion afterward that really makes the experience indelible. Otherwise, it is just another piece of entertainment…and <u>maybe</u> a conversation piece for a few minutes before the crowd moves on to whatever is next for them.

The stunt is art imitating life, but it is the potential for change in behavior that may be more like life imitating (or NOT imitating) the artistry that was just presented.

If you would like to see these kinds of skits in action, you can search for them using keywords such as those I have reflected above. You may also do so via the following links if they are still functional:

https://www.youtube.com/watch?v=3p4gD5rurdo
https://www.youtube.com/watch?v=69gDJQ_L74A
https://www.youtube.com/watch?v=6w7bU_-bFpo

FINALLY

We are talking about flexible, creative, relevant, improvisational, live theater—with the LIVE aspects of performance clearly more impactful than many other art forms which convey meaning. We are also talking about times of change in our world that some say are almost as fast as the speed of brainwaves themselves. And with such rapid change, Eric Hoffer's assertion that learners inherit the earth is even more compelling. We certainly don't want to discover that we are among the knowledgeable folks who find themselves exquisitely prepared for life in a world that has disappeared and left an unfamiliar one in its place.

If rehabilitation is about restoring folks to a *former* excellence, what do we do with those who are still trying to *reach* excellence? Stephen Glenn says we provide opportunities for people to become apprentices for life. We expose them to vehicles of <u>habilitation</u> to prepare them for successful living.

"Imitation of Life" as a model of what some call "edu-tainment" is a proven vehicle for art imitating life, and ultimately for life to become more effectively <u>shaped</u> by the art that is an inspired vision of life displayed on stage. Perhaps Dostoevsky is correct about ultimate outcomes, and you can be part of creating experiences to help shape

IMITATION OF LIFE

a world in which life can draw the very reason for its existence from the art that folks like you will manifest.

Are you ready?
Willing?
Able?
Needed?
Yes! Believe it!

Let's allow Herman Melville to have the last word of encouragement for you…with a brief quote from Mohandas Gandhi as an endnote, which you will likely find familiar:

> **"We cannot live only for ourselves. A thousand fibers connect us with our fellow men; and among those fibers, as sympathetic threads, our actions run as causes, and they come back to us as effects."**
>
> **"Be the change you wish to see in the world."**
> Produce imitations of life!

GETTING TO KNOW ROB SIMON

Rob Simon is a veteran educator, trainer, consultant and speaker/performer working with school systems and various agencies coast to coast. Through his own POSITIVE RHYTHM PRODUCTIONS, he produces and directs topical workshop, classroom, assembly, keynote, theater-related, storytelling, and other creative presentations for diverse audiences, using various training models, persuasive speech, original songs, characterizations, essays, poetry, and more.

As of the date of this publication, Rob is also working on a special project as the Restorative Practices Advocate for West High School in Wichita, Kansas, where his efforts are part of a campaign to establish restorative justice in schools to reverse what many call the "school to prison pipeline" that is energized by traditional punitive discipline in schools.

Rob holds a BS in Social Studies from Texas College in Tyler, Texas an MA in Communication from Wichita State University, and certification or experience in numerous educational training models.

Since the 1980s, Rob has consciously redefined himself as an educator and has discovered and modeled many strategies to help "draw forth" the best from thousands of people with whom he has worked. Rob considers his work the pursuit of a personal mission, which he says is to "ignite within all of us…the desire and the power to live a highly fruitful life."

Rob has successfully promoted and employed the "Imitation of Life" approach to facilitate significant learning through creative theatrical presentations regularly since his career began in the 1970s. With much of his work today, he continues to use the performing arts as strategy to educate in an entertaining way.

For more information, contact Rob:

Positive Rhythm Productions
1736 Womer Drive
Wichita, Kansas 67203-1538
(316) 945-7622
www.positiverhythm.org
info@positiverhythm.org

INDEX

A

ABC 6
Abramovic, Maria 122
Academic goals 63
Adams, Patch 122
Adaptive action method 81
Addison, Laura 97
African 106, 107, 108, 113, 117, 119, 129
African-American 16, 25, 105, 106, 107, 115, 118, 126
African religions 109
Alder, Shannon 77
Alternatives 64, 65, 66, 68, 160
Amin, Idi 129
Anchor 28, 38, 39, 40, 41
Anderson, Walter 27
Angelou, Maya 41, 42, 85
Anonymous 58
Another Brick In The Wall 159
Armstrong, Kristin 87
Arts As Meaning Makers... 127
Arts integration 126, 132
Asimov, Isaac 84
Atom 16, 17

B

Bach, Richard 100
Back-To-School Special 88, 90, 94, 97
Bagger Vance 18
Baudelaire, Charles 122
Beautiful Boy 18
Bell, Joshua 166
Bennett, Roy T. 86
Bennett, William 74
Big Fat Monster 92, 98, 99
Bissinger, H.G. 162
Bitch 53, 54, 142, 145, 147
Black female pilots 107
Black Like Me 162
Bly, Nellie 168
Boy/Girl pairs 145
Brooks Junior High 61
Brooks, Terry X, 7
Brost, Akiroq 27
Brown, Asa Don 27
Brown, Brene' 27
Brown, Chris 139
Bryant, Kobe 27
Buckner TAPS V, 123
Burke, Edmund 112, 148
Burton, Tim 77
Buscaglia, Leo 85
Byrd, Annette 75

C

Calahan, Joseph M. 76
Caldwell, Thomas 24
Caletti, Deb 8
Campbell, Joseph 86
Candid Camera 162, 168
Cantor 11, 12
Caribbean Connection 108, 109
Carlin, George 77
Catchafire 108
Chains to Wings 107
Choose Respect 138, 139
Close, Del 46, 56
Coben, Harlan 96
Cohen, Leonard 122
Collingwood, R.G. 100
Columbia Journalism Review 166
Common ground 12, 15
Conceptual Outline 65
Confronting dating abuse 136
Confucius 74
Connection 23, 28, 35, 37, 106
Cooke, Christian 122
Cornett, Claudia 127
Creating Original Opera 129
Creative theater VIII, 4, 18, 26. 27, 76, 85, 88, 89, 107, 124, 129, 132, 139, 153, 154, 155
Creative theatrics 4, 64, 89, 149, 165
Cultural arts 105, 106, 113
Cultural Arts Camp 105, 106
Cultural diversity 106, 108
Cyrillic 110, 111

D

Da Vinci, Leonardo 86, 122
Degas, Edgar 58
De Lint, Charles X
Disadvantage 68, 105
Do what you can… 153
Dostoevsky, Fyodor X, 158, 170
Dragon to Butterfly 11, 12
Dream Invader 92
Dreyfuss, Richard 18
Drucker, Peter 97
Drumming 109, 113, 119
Du Sautoy, Marcus X

E

Educate and engage 138
Education-based clients 63
Edu-tainment 170
Edwin Laughing Fox 77
Einstein, Albert 85, 122
Eliot, George 83, 122
Emerson, Roger 114
Emotional whiplash 69
Evaluation 97, 128, 130, 139
[Exercises] to Connect Artistry 132, 133, 134

F

"Face Down" 142
Family Violence Prevention Fund 163, 168
Farmers 120
Feuillerat, Rachelle 136
Folktales 106, 108
Ford, Harrison 18
Foster, Carl 28
Frankl, Viktor E. 86
Franklin, Benjamin 78

Friday Night Lights 162
Fugitive, The 18
Fuller, R. Buckminster 148
Funt, Allen 162

G

Gandhi, Mohandas 27, 171
Gang 17, 54
General Principles for [Arts] Integration 131
Giovanni, Nikki 87
Glenn, H. Stephen X, 158, 170
Gonzales, Ed 21, 25
Gopnik, Alison 97
Gracy, Macyn 136, 140, 141
Greene, Ellen 97
Greene, Jay P. 158, 161
Grey, Jennifer 136
Griffin, John Howard 172
Griots Storytelling Institute 105
Griots, The 105, 106

H

Habilitation 158, 170
Halsell, Grace 162
Hamlet X
Hepburn, Audrey
Hertzog, Jodi 140
Highest Common Denominator 149
History to current events 62
Hoffer, Eric 158, 170
Hopper, Edward 58
House of Mirrors 31
Human Systems Dynamics 81

I

I See The Rhythm 126
Ideals 159
If not you… 148
I'm Going Crazy 90
Imitate life X, 4, 125
Imitation of life VII, IX, 6, 21, 22, 25, 27, 40, 46, 59, 61, 62, 64, 65, 67, 82, 87, 123, 129, 168, 170, 174
Improv 46, 47, 48, 49, 51, 52, 57, 58, 59, 61, 68, 75, 76, 77, 89, 111, 145
Improv troupe 139
Improvisation[al] 49, 51, 52, 57, 63, 65, 74, 76, 79, 81, 82, 87, 152, 170
Inappropriate Rap 93
Indirect experience VII
Information VIII, 20, 51, 66, 68, 71, 127, 155
Instrumental music 73
Integrate the arts 122, 127, 128
Interdisciplinary 125
Interruptive stunts/theater 6, 162, 168
IOL 64, 65, 66, 99, 100
Issues and Society 129

J

Janssen, David 18
Johnson, Jimmy 87
Johnson, Nick 124
Jones, Tommy Lee 18

K

Karate Kid 113
Kazantzakis, Nikos 86

Kennedy, John F. 100, 161
Kennedy, Mimi 87
Kilmister, Lemmy 8
King Jr., Martin Luther 88
Klan 10, 11, 12
Kluger, Jeffrey 87
Kolb's Model of Learning 80
Kubler-Ross, Elizabeth 85

L

Law & Order 168
Lennon, John 18
Lewis, C.S. 82
Lewis, Daniel Day 122
Life Imitates Art 158, 159
Light stage/dark stage 32
Lincoln, Nebraska 12
Literacy 105
Living for Tomorrow 45
Love, Not Lies
Lubbock, John 83
Luther, Martin 58
"Lying" Nun 18
Lynn, Cheryl 27

M

Magic Mirror 30, 31, 32
Mahalia 21, 25
Male dominated society 25
Mann, Terrence 8
Marshall, Alfred 77
Masters of the Hormones 92
Maurois, Andre 100
Mead, Margaret 148
Meaning and excellence 84, 85
Melville, Herman 171
Methoxsalen 162
Michaels, Mia 73

Millman, Dan 11, 112
Mime 2, 75, 124, 127, 145
Mimesis VII, 1, 3, 6
Mirror X, 28, 31, 32, 87
Model humans 25
Montessori, Maria 96
Mork and Mindy 9
Mr. Holland's Opus 18
Multi-talented 60
Music VIII, 12, 38, 60, 61, 63, 64, 74, 75, 76, 77, 93, 101, 102, 104, 109, 111, 114, 119, 122, 124, 126, 127, 128, 134, 151, 163, 167

N

Nascent prophecy 11, 12
New York Metropolitan Opera 129
Nietzsche, Friedrich 77
No Difference In The Dark 15, 16
No Room In The Heart 114
Not By The Sword 12
Nuclear 83

O

Obama, Barack 75
O'Keefe, Georgia 58
Oliver, John 46
Ostegard, Paul 75

P

Palahniuk, Chuck 100
Peaceful Warrior, The 111, 112
Pectopah 110
Peer influence 5, 54, 65, 92, 137, 138, 163

Phone abuse 168
Picasso, Pablo 122, 123
Pink Floyd 159
Planting Seeds 124
Plato 58
Poetry VIII, 122, 126, 127, 128, 173
Positive rhythm 99
Positive Rhythm Productions 173, 174
Positive social change 3
Powell, Eleanor
Powell, John Joseph 27
Pratchett, Terry 8
Prevention programming 64
Process of reflection 81
Processing 6, 49, 68, 70, 78, 81, 82, 84, 85, 87, 141, 147
Pryor, Richard 129

Q

Queen Mother 115, 116, 117
Quiñones, John 164, 165

R

Rap 96, 97, 100, 111, 127, 134, 160
R.E.A.D 109
Real life VIII, 11, 27, 40, 53, 57, 84, 156, 164
Real world VII, X, 3, 6, 7, 40, 77, 104
Red Jumpsuit Apparatus, The 142, 143
Redford, Robert 148, 156
Reid, Tim 16
Relationship violence 137
Rihanna 139
Riley, Richard 75
RJOY 139
Road rage 56
Robbins, Tony 86
Robot, The 61
Roosevelt, Eleanor 87
Rosenhan, David 168
Roth, David 12
RTI International 139
Rubenstein, David 122
Russell, Bertrand 82
Russian proverb 11

S

Saggin' 160
Scenarios 56, 58, 163
Schiller, Phil 96
Schlesinger Jr., Arthur M. 161
Schoolhouse Rock 125
Secret Life of Prince Charming 8
Secretary of Education 76, 77
Seeds of Greatness 115, 119, 120, 123
Sesame Street 125
Seven Times 144
Shakespeare, William X
Shelton, Jon Noel 21
Shoplift(ing) 68, 69, 96, 164
Showcase scene 49
Simon, Denise Jackson- 124
Simon, Rob 173
Sirk, Douglas 21, 25
Sister Veronica 19, 20
Skill and Talent Building 132
Skills 64, 65
Smith, Will 18
Smithrim, Katharine 127

Smorgasbord of subject matter 67
Smoove, J.B. 45, 55
Smrhyne 21
Snow White 27
Social policy 64, 65
Sorkin , Aaron X
Soul Sister 162
St. Denis, Ruth 58
Start Strong 53, 137, 138, 139, 141
Start Strong Wichita 51, 137, 139, 144
Steiner, Rudolph 87
Still, I Rise 41, 42, 43, 44
Stone, Emma 46, 57
Strahler, Samantha 141, 142
Straw dog argument 73
Stunt 140, 162, 163, 167, 168, 170
Suess, Dr. 148, 156
Swardson, Nick 46

T

Taffel, Ron 87
Talent show 27, 29
Talent survey 29
TAP 139, 141, 144
Teaching About and In The Arts 130
Teaching Through the Arts 131
Teaching the Arts Performing School 123
Teens About Prevention 136, 139
Terry Ellen 122
That's Not Cool 168
Theme show 30, 31, 33
Tooele, Utah 73
Torn scene 53
Trapp, Larry 12
Triple threat 60
Truth songs 71
Turner, Lana 21

U

Unamuno, Miguel 85
Upstanders 141
Upward Bound 28. 33, 45
Utah 47

V

Valley Girl 160
Van Noten, Dries 100
Venus Flytrap 16
Vicariously 7
Visual art element 74

W

Warhol, Andy 85
Watterson, Kathryn 12
Weingarten, Gene 166, 167
Weinstein, Lori 136
Weiss, Daniel 166, 167
Weisser, Michael 12
Welch, Jack 158
Wesley, John 148
What if 89
What? SO what? NOW what? 79, 80, 81
What Would You Do? 6, 164
Whipple, Chris 168
Whose Line Is It Anyway? 49
Wichita State University 29, 124, 140, 173
Wilde, Oscar 158

Williams, Robin 9, 11, 18, 46, 57
Winter, Ronnie 143
Wooden, John 158

Y

You Here Now 154
You Tube 17, 18, 63, 144, 168, 170

Z

Zacharias, Ravi X, 158
Zwick, Edward 96

www.ingramcontent.com/pod-product-compliance
Lightning Source LLC
Chambersburg PA
CBHW020242010526
44107CB00039B/1464/J